HOW TO BE SUCCESSFUL AT SPONSORSHIP SALES

By Sylvia Allen and C. Scott Amann

1

ABOUT THE AUTHORS

Sylvia Allen

MANAGEMENT:
- Leads one of the country's top marketing organizations in the field of sports and special events, founded in 1978.
- Led agency to be named one of 50 fastest-growing companies in NJ by leading area business publication.
- Held successively more responsible communications positions with Fortune 500 companies including McGraw-Hill and AT&T.
- Co-founded professional organization, Women in Sports and Events (WISE).
- Program Developer and Manager for Sports, Event and Entertainment Marketing program at New York University's Management Institute.
- Founded and managed Vail International Multi-Image Festival.
- Founded and managed American Sandsculpting Championship.

MARKETING:
- Developed marketing, public relations, advertising and sponsorship programs for a diversity of clients including QwestDex, AT&T, the Garden State Arts Center, Pan American Sports Corporation, a wide range of Downtown Improvement Associations, San Gennaro Festival in New York City, Comcast Cable and New Jersey Broadcasters Association.
- Currently Adjunct Associate Professor of Marketing at New York University.
- Wrote and delivered over one thousand seminars on marketing and sponsorship throughout the world.

ACADEMIC:
- New York University, Management Institute: Adjunct Associate Professor of Marketing and Program Advisor (17 years)
- International Institute for Research: Workshop Leader (10 years)
- American Marketing Association: Workshop Leader
- The Conference Board: Panel Discussion Leader (2 years)
- National Main Street Program: Workshop Leader (10 years)
- Brookdale College: How to Build a Successful Consulting Business (18 years)
- New School for Social Research: Adjunct Assistant Professor
- International Festivals and Events Association (7 years)

PUBLISHED WORKS:	• Author: **A Manager's Guide to Audio Visuals** (McGraw-Hill) • Author: **How to Prepare a Production Budget for Film & Videotape** (McGraw-Hill) • Author: **How to Be Successful at Sponsorship Sales** • Contributing author: **The Nonprofit Manager's Handbook** (Wiley) • Contributing author: **The Nonprofit Handbook (Fundraising)** (Wiley) • Contributing writer: **Event Management News; Brandweek, Sponsorship Opportunities Newsletter; Fund Raising Management; Sales and Marketing Strategies News; National Main Street News; Sport Travel; Radio Ink; Radio Advertising Bureau (RAB); Special Events Magazine; iE; Downtown Promotion Report; NJ Biz** • Author of numerous magazine and newspaper articles about marketing, management and sponsorship.
BOARD POSITIONS (PAST/PRESENT):	• Co-founder, Women in Sports and Events (**WISE**) • Advisory Board, National Sports Marketing Network • Past President, Jersey Shore Public Relations and Advertising Association • Past President, Tower Hill Choir • Past Chair, Marketing Advisory Committee, Family and Children's Service • Board Member, Monmouth County Arts Council • Chair, Sponsorship Committee, The Solomon R. Guggenheim Museum • Member, Business Advisory Committee, Guggenheim • Past Vice President, Board of Directors, Bike New York • Past President, Asbury Park Repertory Theatre Company • Member, Players Club • Founder, Sylvia's Children
EDUCATION:	• MA, Empire State College, Culture and Policy, Cum Laude • BA, University of Minnesota, Speech/Theatre Arts

Sylvia Allen has provided seminars, workshops and lectures for a variety of national organizations including the National Main Street program, The Conference Board, the American Management Association and International Festivals and Events Association as well as hundreds of speeches for a wide range of local, regional, national and international associations and organizations.

C. Scott Amann

Scott Amann has his own private practice representing television producers and screenwriters. Most notable of his accomplishments are the negotiation and administration of a television production deal with TNT for a 2X Cable Ace Award-winning sports documentary entitled "Mohammed Ali - The Whole Story" and the cable presentation entitled "Family Values: The Mob and the Movies."

Mr. Amann serves as a legal and event management consultant to several amateur and professional organizations including, but not restricted to, the following:

- The National City Leagues Association, Inc. a/k/a the National Pro-Am;
- Atlanta Committee for the 1996 Olympic Games (baseball);
- The United States Basketball League;
- The New England Collegiate Baseball League, and
- The Westchester County Center.

Mr. Amann also was General Counsel for Titan Sports, Inc., owners of the World Wrestling Federation. In this position he was directly responsible for the negotiation and contract administration of the following:

- Consumer product licenses;
- Talent/wrestler's booking contracts;
- Domestic/international television broadcasts rights, including all pay-per-views, cable programs and home video releases; and
- Any and all other legal issues affecting the day to day operation of a two hundred plus (200+) employee sports/entertainment organization.

Mr. Amann serves as an Assistant Professor of Marketing Manage at New York University teaching sports law, event management/marketing law, and the legal issues of licensing as well as having his own private law practice specializing in entertainment, events and sports law.

Introduction ... How to Get Started

In the 60's and 70's sponsorship was a linear relationship where a corporation gladly gave money for tickets to a performance or banner exposure. The sponsors handed the money to the sport or event, got their benefits, and were happy. That is no longer true. Today's sponsors are highly sophisticated and recognize that sponsorship is just another media component of their marketing mix. As a result, sponsorships must have a variety of components including media, cross-marketing opportunities, promotions, partnership recommendations, and event extensions to get the greatest return on investment.

This book will provide you with the tools you need to be successful at sponsorship sales. Briefly, the specific steps involved are as follows:

1. Take inventory of your property (what do you have to sell);

2. Solicit and secure media partners through barter by making them sponsors of the event;

3. Incorporate the media components into the sponsorship offerings;

4. Develop one page "sell" fact sheet;

5. Determine the various levels of participation based on inventory;

6. Solicit sponsors through the following steps:

    •Research sponsors (annual reports, on-line data search, etc.);
    •Call and pre-qualify at the highest possible level;
    •Send fact sheet;
    •Follow up with call/set appointment;
    •Meet with sponsors and determine levels of commitment;
    •Help sponsors integrate this sponsorship into their current marketing plan;
    •Get commitment and go to contract;
    •Get initial down payment;
    •Work with sponsors on participation;
    •Attend event and manage sponsorship;
    •Send post-event report;
    •Follow through and renew for next year.

Sounds simple, doesn't it! And, it can be if you follow the principles offered in this book. These sponsorship strategies and tactics have been used in communities of 1,500 people and for events that attract millions. The techniques are the same. If you follow these instructions and concepts you will definitely have more success than you have ever experienced before. Good luck!

Chapter 1 - 12 STEPS TO SPONSORSHIP SUCCESS

Selling sponsorships is not a matter of buying a mailing list of potential buyers, writing a direct mail letter, putting together a "package", mailing everything out and waiting for the telephone to ring with people offering you money. It's a nice dream but the reality is much more complicated (and time consuming) than that.

Before getting started you should have a definition of sponsorship. The following definition is by no means perfect; however, there are some choice words that help you purse your sponsorship sales with a good foundation.

Sponsorship is an investment, in cash or in kind, in return for access to exploitable business potential associated with an event or highly publicized entity.

The key words in this definition are "investment", "access to", and "exploitable". First, investment. By constantly looking at sponsorship as an investment opportunity, where there is a viable payback, no longer are you talking to someone about a payment of cash or money. Rather, use the word **investment** that automatically implies value will be returned to the investor. Second, **access to** which means having the ability to be associated with a particular offering (event, sport, festival, fair ... you name it). Lastly, **exploitable**, a positive word which means, "to take the greatest advantage of" the relationship. In other words, allowing sponsors to make the greatest use of their investment and capitalize on their relationship.

With this definition in mind you can now go forward and take the 12 steps to sponsorship success. If you take these basic 12 steps you will be assured of greater success in your sponsorship endeavors. These basic steps, and the components that comprise each of them, are covered in depth in this book. References are made throughout this chapter to the specific chapters that go into the specific references in detail.

Step 1 ... Take inventory

What are you selling? You have a number of elements in your event that have value to the sponsor. They include, but are not restricted to, the following:

- Radio, TV and print partners
- Retail outlet
- Collateral material ... posters, flyers, brochures, table tents
- Banners
- Tickets: quantity for giving to sponsor plus ticket backs for redemption
- VIP seating
- VIP parking
- Hospitality ... for the trade, for customers, for employees
- On-site banner exposure
- Booth
- Audio announcements
- Payroll stuffers

8

- Billboards
- Product sales/product displays
- Celebrity appearances/interviews
- Internet exposure

And, you can think of more. Look at your event as a store and take inventory of the many things that will have value to your sponsors, whether it is for the marketing value or hospitality value. Take your time in making up this list … time spent at the beginning will be rewarded by more effective sponsorships when you get into the selling process.

Step 2 …Develop your media and retail partners

Next, approach your media and retail partners. (SEE CHAPTERS 12-18) They should be treated the same way as all other sponsors, with the same rights and benefits. In fact, after taking your inventory, steps two and three are done almost simultaneously as you must have something to give to your potential media and retail partners that describes the sponsorship. Briefly, here's what is important to these two key partners.

Media

Your event offers the media an opportunity to increase their non-traditional revenue (NTR). You have an audience, sampling opportunities, sales opportunities and multiple media exposures that the media people can offer to their own advertisers. Many times an advertiser asks for additional merchandising opportunities from the media. Your event offers them that opportunity. You can let them sell a sponsorship for you in return for the airtime or print coverage. Just make sure it is always coordinated through you so they are not approaching your sponsors and you are not approaching their advertisers. From radio and TV you want airtime that can then be included in your sponsorship offerings. From print you want ad space and/or an advertorial (a special section). In both instances you are getting valuable media to include in your sponsorship offerings to your potential sponsors.

Treat your media just like your other sponsors. Give them the attendant benefits that go with the value of their sponsorship. When the event is over, they should provide you with proof of performance (radio and TV, an affidavit of performance; print should give you tear sheets) and, conversely, you should provide them with a post event report (SEE CHAPTER 39).

Retail

A retail partner … supermarket, drugstore, fast food outlet … offers you some additional benefits that can be passed on to your sponsors. And, with a retail outlet, you can approach manufacturers and offer them some of these benefits. For example, once you have a retail partner the following opportunities exist:

- End cap or aisle displays
- Register tape promotions
- In-store displays
- Store audio announcements

- Inclusion in weekly flyers
- Weekly advertising
- Cross-promotion opportunities
- Bag stuffers
- Placemats (fast food outlets)
- Shopping bags
- On-pack promotions
- On-floor promotions

Again, as with the media, even though this might be straight barter, treat the retail outlets as you would a paying sponsor. They are providing you with terrific benefits that can be passed on to your other sponsors, a tremendous value in attracting retail products. And, as with the media, have them provide you with documentation of their support ... samples of bags, flyers, inserts, etc. In return, you will provide them with a post-event report, documenting the benefits they received and the value of those benefits.

Step 3 ... Develop your sponsorship offerings

Now you can put together the various components of your sponsorship offerings so you are prepared to offer valuable sponsorships. Try to avoid too many levels and too "cutesy" headings. Don't use gold, silver and bronze. Don't use industry-specific terms your buyer might not understand. For example, if a baseball sponsorship: first base, home run, etc. (If buyers don't understand the words they probably won't take a look at the offering!). Simply, you can have title, presenting, associate, product specific and event specific categories. They are easy to understand and easy to sell. Of course, title is the most expensive and most effective. Think of the Volvo Tennis Classic or the Virginia Slims Tennis Classic. The minute the name of your event is "married" to the sponsor's name the media have to give the whole title. Great exposure for your title sponsor. (SEE CHAPTER 11 - How to Price Your Event Components).

The first step you will take in preparing for your initial sponsor contact is to prepare a one page fact sheet that clearly and succinctly outlines the basics of your event (the who, what, where, when of your property) and highlights the various benefits of being associated with that event (radio, TV, print, on-site, etc.). (SEE CHAPTER 7 - Sponsorship Fact Sheet).

Step 4 ... Research your sponsors

Learn about your potential sponsors. Get on the Internet, read the annual reports, do a data search on the company, use the many sourcebooks that are available ... find out what the companies are currently sponsoring, what their branding strategies are, what their business objectives are. Become an expert on your prospects ... the more you know about them the better prepared you will be for their questions and the easier it will be for you to craft a sponsorship offering that meets their specific needs.

Step 5 ... Do initial sponsor contact

Then, pick up the telephone. Try to reach the proper person (SEE CHAPTER 4, Where to Find Sponsorship Dollars). When you reach the correct person, don't launch right into a sales pitch. Rather, ask them several questions about their business that will indicate to you whether or not they are a viable sponsor for you project. (If you've done your homework, the answer will be "yes" and you can continue.)

Step 6 ... Go for the appointment

Once you have had a brief discussion, try to get the appointment. If they say, "Send me a 'package,'" respond with "I'll do even better than that. I've prepared a succinct one page Fact Sheet that highlights the various marketing and promotion components of my event. Do you want me to send it to you via facsimile or e-mail?" Then, ask for the fax number or e-mail address, send it to them right away and then call back shortly to make sure they received it. If they have received it go for the appointment. Explain that the fact sheet is merely a one-dimensional outline that cannot begin to describe the total event and you would like to meet with them, at their convenience, to show them pictures, previous press coverage, a video ... whatever you have. Follow the basic sales techniques of choices ...Monday or Friday, morning or afternoon. Don't give them a chance to say they can't see you.

Step 7 ... Be creative

Once in front of the sponsor, be prepared. Demonstrate your knowledge of their business by offering a sponsorship that meets their specific needs. Help them come up with a new and unique way to enhance their sponsorship beyond the event. For example, if it's a pet store, come up with a contest that involves the customers and their pets. Or, devise a contest where people have to fill out an entry form to win something. Think about hospitality opportunities ... rewards for leading salespeople, special customer rewards, incentives for the trade. Be prepared to offer these ideas, and more, to help the sponsor understand how this sponsorship offers him/her great benefit.

Step 8 ... Make the sale

The moment of truth ... you have to ask for the sale. You can't wait for the sponsor to offer; rather you have to ask, "Will we be working together on this project?" or something like that. You will have to develop your own closing questions. Hopefully, as you went through the sales process, you determined their needs and developed a program to meet those needs. And, you certainly should have done enough questioning to determine what their level of participation would be. Keep in mind that different personality styles buy differently which means you must select from a variety of closing techniques to ensure the right "fit" with the different personalities.

As with any sale, once you have concluded the sale, follow up with a detailed contract that outlines each party's obligations. A handshake is nice but if the various elements aren't spelled out there can be a bad case of "but you said" when people sometimes hear what they *want* to hear, not necessarily what was spoken. (SEE CHAPTERS 69-73). Make sure you include a payment schedule that ensures you receive all your money before the event. If not, you could suffer from the "call girl principle".

Step 9 … Keep the sponsor in the loop

Once you have gone through the sales process you want to keep your sponsor involved up to, and through, your event. See if their public relations department will put out a press release on their involvement. Show them the event collateral as it is being developed to make sure they are happy with their logo placement. (With fax and e-mail this is now a very simple process.) Make sure they are kept up-to-date on new sponsors, new activities … whatever is happening. The more you involve them in the process the more involved (and committed) they become.

Step 10 … Involve the sponsor in the event

Make sure your sponsor is involved in the event. Don't let a sponsor hand you a check and say, "Let me know what happens". You are doomed to failure. Get them to participate by being on site … walk around with them … discuss their various banner locations, the quality of the audience, the lines at their booth, whatever is appropriate to their participation. (SEE CHAPTER 37, "Managing Sponsorship on Site for Guaranteed Results").

Step 11 … Provide sponsors with a post-event report

There's a very old saying regarding presentations: "Tell them what you are going to tell them, tell them, then tell them what you told them." The post-event report is the last segment of this saying. Provide your sponsors with complete documentation of their participation. This should include copies of all collateral material, affidavit of performance from your radio and TV partners, tear sheets, retail brochures, tickets, banners, press stories… whatever has their company name and/or logo prominently mentioned or displayed. This should all be included in a kit, with a written post-event report that lists the valuation of the various components, and presented to the sponsor with a certificate of appreciation for their participation. (SEE CHAPTER 39, Developing the Post-Event Report).

Step 12 … Renew for next year

Now, if you've followed these 12 steps carefully, renewal is easy. In fact, you can get your sponsor to give you a verbal renewal during your event (if it is going well) and certainly after you have provided that sponsor with a post-event report that documents the value of all the marketing components he/she received. You should try for a three to one (3:1) return on their investment. In many instances it will be even more than that if you have delivered as promised.

Conclusion

Selling isn't easy; however, if you follow these 12 steps it will be easier because you will have done your homework and will be prepared to discuss the sponsorship intelligently. These 12 steps make selling fun!

Chapter 2 – GUARANTEED SPONSORS FOR ANY EVENT

Sometimes it's hard to know where to start when soliciting sponsorships. Here is a list of the top 22 potential sponsors you can approach for almost any event.

1. Local electronics retailer;
2. Local beer bottler;
3. Local soft drink bottler;
4. Local banks;
5. Local restaurant association;
6. Local retailers' association;
7. Car dealers;
8. Automobile aftermarket;
9. Long distance carriers;
10. Wireless telephone companies;
11. Network marketing companies (Amway, Nu Skin, Mary Kaye, etc.);
12. Craftspeople;
13. Antique dealers;
14. Fresh produce dealers (mini-Farmer's Markets);
15. Local radio;
16. Local cable;
17. Local newspapers;
18. Local magazines;
19. Food vendors;
20. T-Shirt vendors;
21. Flea market vendors.
22. Mobile marketing agencies

Happy hunting!

Chapter 3 – FACTORS AFFECTING SPONSORSHIP DECISIONS

First and foremost, sponsorship participation is a business decision. Yes, the CEO still exerts influence on sponsorship involvement but no longer is it done emotionally but, rather, on a business basis with measurable objectives.

Second, sponsorship decisions are not made on the spur of the moment nor are they made based upon someone sending a proposal to a prospective sponsor and having that person, just based on the proposal, making a decision to become a sponsor. In sponsorship solicitation and sales it is very much like a courtship where each party wants to get to know the other better before joining together.

Depending upon dollar amounts involved, sponsorship decisions can take years. For those of us involved in the sales process one of the best traits one can have is tenacity! Basically, the sponsorship decision process involves a number of people at different levels with each assuming responsibility for one particular segment of the process, depending upon objectives for involvement and dollars involved. For example, it is entirely possible for the Director of Marketing, Sales Manager, Merchandising Manager, Public Relations Director and Human Relations Manager to each have some involvement in making a sponsorship decision. Each would want to study the sponsorship proposal to determine what elements, if any, impact their particular department's goals.

When selling sponsorships, keep in mind that the prime objective of the proposal is to whet the sponsor's appetite. Hopefully, you will have made initial contact with the potential sponsor to discuss his/her needs to ensure that your proposal is well suited to these needs. Then, you will have sent a brief summation of the proposal, highlighting those issues previously discussed and emphasizing how the various marketing/sales/ promotional opportunities dovetail with their current strategies in these areas. Last, you would try to get an appointment with the sponsor to discuss, in detail, how your program works and what sponsorship opportunities there are.

What should be in your package? It should contain the following:

1. Media exposure (dollar value/ratings/readership, etc.);

2. Marketing/merchandising/sales opportunities;

3. Hospitality rights including tickets, VIP parking, etc.;

4. Product exclusivity issue;

5. Signage, on-site exposure (audio billboards, banners, etc.);

6. Listing of other participating sponsors;

7. Brief history of the event/sport/venue/facility;

8. Testimonial letters from previous sponsors.

All of that information should be typed, double spaced, and not be more than eight pages. Remember that the person receiving your proposal gets hundreds, if not thousands, of these proposals annually. The time spent on each one will be minimal and your proposal must stand out if it is to be noticed. If it is brief, and well written, with the sponsor's objectives in mind, you will quickly get to the next step … meeting and discussion.

Prior to that meeting learn all you can about your potential sponsors. What sponsorships have they done in the past? What are their corporate mission statements? If they are a public company, read their annual report. Do a data search at the library to discover how this organization approaches their market; what is their advertising strategy; who are their customers; what is their product line. In short, you want to be as knowledgeable as the person you will be meeting with so you can discuss how your sponsorship program is so well suited to their organization.

Make sure you send a written summary after each meeting that outlines your discussion and reiterates how the sponsorship opportunity presented is appropriate. Be thorough in your follow-through and be consistent in your presentation of facts and figures. When you get a sponsorship commitment, write a contract that clearly, and carefully, outlines the terms of the contract and how each party benefits. This is your implementation road map and needs to be as accurate as possible. Then, deliver 110% and renewal will be hard to pass up!

Chapter 4 – WHERE TO PLACE SPONSORSHIP DOLLARS (from the sponsor's point of view)

Whether investing in local, regional, national or global markets, sponsors have some basic questions that need answering before they can make a decision on their participation. Here are eight questions that can help narrow the choices of where to place sponsorship dollars:

1. Will the sponsorship drive sales?

2. Will it enhance or reinforce brand image?

3. Will it increase awareness of the company's product, brand, or service?

4. Will it provide retail and trade tie-ins?

5. Will it drive volume and long-term profitability?

6. Will it increase share of the market?

7. Will it provide a vehicle for entertaining clients?

8. Can it differentiate the product or brand from a competitor's?

9. Will it give the company a competitive edge, i.e., exposure in a market the competition is not in?

Then, once these questions have been asked, screen and grade the choices to make a selection by using the following seven questions:

1. Is the objective corporate or brand specific?

2. Is it a one-time event or a long-term commitment?

3. Do the locations and dates fit company needs?

4. How many attendees can be expected (total exposure of brand/product)?

5. Will there be co-sponsors?

6. Will the company be lost in a crowd of other sponsors?

7. What is the cost relative to the expected return?

When developing your sponsorship proposals, keep the sponsor in mind and remember that these questions will be part of the consideration process. Understanding the company and these questions before making a sponsorship solicitation will pave the way for a more effective, and more successful, sponsorship presentation.

Chapter 5 – WHERE TO FIND SPONSORSHIP DOLLARS

If you are involved in sponsorship sales, you often feel like you are looking for a needle in a haystack. Many times you don't have a contact name nor do you know what department has responsibility for sponsorship, so you start cold calling. Don't despair. You can find sponsorship dollars if you are persistent and consistent.

Sponsorship dollars can be found in a variety of departments within a company and under a range of corporate titles. Of course, when you initially contact a company, the first person you will ask to speak to is the person in charge of sponsorship for that organization. And, if they have a sponsorship department (and more companies are adding them daily), you are quickly and easily connected to the right department. Now, do you talk to the Director, Vice President, or Manager of that department? It depends upon the corporate culture and how responsibilities are assigned to different titles. Hopefully, before calling, you will have done your homework and determined the culture and know the appropriate person to talk to.

Other calls you make won't be that easy. Sometimes sponsorship dollars reside in the marketing budget; other times in public relations. With consumer goods, you will often find sponsorship money in brand or product management; other companies may have funds available through human relations or sales. In today's world of highly automated telephone systems, you may have to make several calls to any specific organization before you are able to find the appropriate person.

To make your initial calling easier, read the various trade publications addressed to event marketers. You should really keep back issues of these publications and use them as resource material when researching who is spending sponsorship dollars on what. Of course, with the Internet, data retrieval has become much easier. At least you now have a name for your initial contact and, even if they are no longer involved, they can refer you to the proper contact person.

Also keep in mind that more than one person can be involved in sponsorships and that more than one department participates in sponsorship. If you have approached the marketing department and, in spite of the quality of your presentation and appropriateness of the event, they have still turned you down, **that doesn't mean you can't go back to that very same company.** Just select another department. If the match of sponsor and event is right, you may be successful going through other channels.

If you are a non-profit organization or have a cause-related affiliation with your event, you can go to the grant administration or charitable contributions department. Keep in mind that these decisions are always made a year in advance, so don't expect short-term monies from these departments. Also, considering that major corporations are bombarded with requests for funding, sponsorship and otherwise, you may not get the sponsorship dollars you want. However, it is better to get some money than none!

In addition to reading the trade publications to find out who is spending what and where, use your professional trade association affiliations as a resource too. Organizations that could help you in your networking to determine which companies are doing sponsorship are local advertising clubs, International Festivals and Events Association and local festivals and events associations, Public Relations Society of America (PRSA), Promotion Marketing Association (PMA), and local broadcaster associations, to name just a few. Attend the meetings, take advantage of networking opportunities and you will be surprised at how much information you can get.

networking

There are also directories that list the various people involved in sponsorship including *IEG Directory of Sponsorship Marketing*, *Team Marketing Sourcebook*, ADWEEK'S *Agency Directory* and *Consumer Products Directory*, the advertising agency's Bible -- *The Red Book*, and EPM's *Entertainment Marketing* and *Licensing Business Sourcebook* . These publications average $200-300 each, but are well worth the investment compared against five-, six- and seven-figure sponsorship sales.

In many instances, the size and type of event determines where you might find sponsorship dollars. For example, if you have a local event that only impacts your local area, you can go to the local distributors or field offices. Often they have discretionary dollars that can be allocated to local sponsorships. So, too, with regional events. Within the last couple of years, Miller Brewing has gone to regional offices where each office can make sponsorship decisions themselves for events within their region. Of course, if your event is national or international, you will still have to go through corporate headquarters for your solicitation.

Whatever channels you go through -- local, regional, national -- start your sponsorship sales process early. Budgets are planned annually; the more lead time you have, the better chance you have of getting your event considered for sponsorship. Don't wait until three months or, worse, three weeks, before the event to start soliciting sponsors. Remember, the greater the lead time, the greater the success rate. Good luck!

Chapter 6 – HOW TO START EVALUATING YOUR PROPERTY

In order to be effective at sponsorship sales, you have to ask yourself some questions before you can prepare a good inventory of "saleable" items. These questions will help you develop sound sponsorship offerings. In many instances these are the same questions your sponsor will ask so going through this exercise will help you be better prepared during the sales call.

1. What are the basics ... where is the event being held, when is it being held, what are the times/dates, what is the estimated attendance? Basically, answer the who-what-when-where-why questions.

2. Is it inside or outside?

3. What are the restrictions of the site/venue? (For example, if your event were being held at the PNC Bank Center you wouldn't be able to bring in another bank as a sponsor. We recently held a concert that was sponsored by Original Coors; the band came with a Budweiser sponsor but had failed to note that in the contract they were prohibited from hanging the Budweiser banner.)

4. Who are your media partners and what portion of that media can be allocated to sponsors (radio, cable, TV, print, billboard, coupons, etc.)?

5. What are the signage capabilities (on-site ... where and how many; horizontal and vertical street banners ... where and how many; other points of visibility ... stage, exhibit area, etc.)?

6. Do you have a retail partner(s)? Who is it? What is the relationship and can they be used for cross promotion?

7. Is the event free or paid admission?

8. Is it a ticketed event? Can the sponsor be on the ticket?

9. What collateral material is planned (posters, flyers, parking passes, etc.)? What visibility will the sponsor have on the collateral material?

10. What are the on-site benefits (audio announcements, banners, signs, posters, booth space, sales space, etc.)?

11. What are the promotional rights (couponing, bouncebacks, register-to-win, product demos, product sampling, etc.)?

12. Are there naming rights (the SPONSOR NAME children's area, the SPONSOR NAME petting zoo, etc.)?

13. Do you have a database of names that can be released to the sponsor?

14. What are the VIP or hospitality opportunities?

15. Will admission tickets be part of the sponsorship offering?

19

16. If there is celebrity involvement, will the sponsor have access to the celebrity?

17. Do you have insurance coverage for the sponsors?

18. What is the sponsor history of the event (good, bad, non-existent, etc.)?

19. Do you have a crisis PR plan in place (particularly necessary for dangerous sports such as offshore powerboat racing, NASCAR racing, etc.)?

20. Is there category exclusivity?

21. If beverage company, can they have pouring rights?

These are the basics. As you look at your own events, I'm sure you can come up with more that are specifically related to your event. However, if you get these 21 questions answered you are well on your way to being able to prepare good, quality sponsorship offerings that will be attractive to corporations who will invest in your event.

Chapter 7 – SPONSORSHIP FACT SHEET

When preparing your material for submission to potential sponsors, keep in mind that they are overworked and understaffed. And, if they are a Fortune 500 company they are deluged with sponsorship requests. The total can be intimidating ... as many as 10,000 a year ... and more! How do you cut through the clutter? How do you get, and keep, their attention? Simply, make your material easy to read and understand.

This simple form can be used for events from 100 to 1,000,000 people. It provides an easy way to summarize the highlights of your sponsorship opportunity, offers the potential sponsor a simple, easy-to-read overview, and facilitates the decision making process. Try it ... it works!

Your one page fact sheet should be just that – only the facts. This includes date of event, title of event, the location, the times, the audience, the marketing opportunities (media partners, etc.) and suggested promotional ideas. You can also list "Sponsorships available up to ...$_____." Don't say "Sponsorships start at $500" because that is all you'll get! You will not make a sale from this sheet. It is merely designed so your prospect can have an overview of your offering. I call it the "appetizer" to whet their appetite for more!

The following page contains a sample one page fact sheet that can help you achieve this objective. See Appendix H for an additional way to get your sponsor involved in the buying process. Appendix H is an Events Benefit Checklist.

OCEANFEST FACT SHEET

LOCATION: Promenade at The Ocean Place Hilton Resort and Spa, Long Branch, NJ

DATES/TIMES: July 4, 10am - 10pm

ATTENDANCE: 250,000+

AUDIENCE: All demographic groups with average attendees 30-45 years old, professional, married with children. Visitors come from all over New Jersey and metro New York.

SPECIFIC ACTIVITIES:
Spectacular fireworks display
VIP reception and priority viewing ..."Evening Under the Stars"
Sports event
Entertainment ...bands, dancing, singing, performance art
Wide range of food selections
Quality arts and crafts

MARKETING OPPORTUNITIES:
Radio, TV, and print coverage (value = $75,000)
Large street banners on Broadway, Joline, Norwood Avenues
Booth space
Audio billboards
Inclusion on posters, flyers, etc. (100,000+)
On-site signage
Table tents
New Jersey Monthly

PROMOTION IDEAS:
Product sampling
Database development(register to win)
Product sales
Contest/promotions
Premium incentives
Couponing/bouncebacks
Cross-promotions/sponsor partnerships

SPONSORSHIP OPTIONS RANGING TITLE SPONSORSHIP TO BOOTH DISPLAYS LET US TAILOR ONE THAT WORKS FOR YOU!

A terrific opportunity to become involved in a community event that attracts over 250,000 people each year from all areas of New Jersey and the Tri-state. One of the premiere events on the Jersey Shore.

Allen Consulting, Inc. 732-946-2711

22

Chapter 8 – BARTER AS PART OF THE SPONSORSHIP MIX

When considering sponsorship, the focus is on dollars - what can be generated and what value the sponsor will receive. Barter, however, is an important element in the sponsorship mix and a good way to offset expenses, particularly in the areas of promotion and media.

Years ago, neighbors bargained over backyard fences -- swapping quilts for homemade preserves, childcare for slipcovers. Manhattan was part of a barter deal of land for beads. Today, barter is big business, with more than $7 billion in goods and services exchanged last year in North America alone. Barter can be an important element in your sponsorship mix.

According to Webster's dictionary, barter is "to trade (e.g., goods, services) without the exchange of money." In sponsorship, barter can be an effective way of offsetting bottom-line expenses and enhancing your event with value-added elements.

The first step in determining barter should be to look at your event budget, line by line, to see which elements are "barter-able." Two of the most common areas in barter are media and promotion. Here's how it works.

A barter relationship is approached like any other sponsorship agreement. The property sales representative approaches a potential sponsor with a benefits package (it's the same package they would present to a sponsor if looking for a cash commitment). Depending upon the level of sponsorship and the desired participation, the sale is negotiated like any other sponsorship *except* that no cash changes hands. For example, if doing a barter deal with a radio station, the station would receive all the sponsor benefits associated with their sponsorship level. Then, the value of that sponsorship would be paid in airtime - radio spots. Now, as the event, you have not only offset the advertising expense in your budget, you have valuable media time that can be incorporated into your sponsorship packages.

In addition to bartering the tangibles - line items that are actual event expenses - you can also barter for intangibles, items that are "nice to have" and enhance your event but were not part of the initial budgeting process.

Barter dollars should be exchanged at retail. Don't ask your barter partner to "cut prices" or "sell it to me wholesale." Be prepared, as with any other sponsor, to demonstrate the retail value of your sponsorship package and how the benefits of your event have intrinsic value, whether the relationship is cash or barter.

Another good barter relationship can be with a supermarket or drug store chain. You can generate positive exposure for your event, the retailer's media and in-store marketing efforts, and you'll also have a retail outlet for other sponsorships. For example, if your sponsorship is with XYZ drug chain and you have a sponsorship opportunity with Gillette, the retail relationship enhances your sponsorship package by giving Gillette a retail outlet that is already involved with your event. The synergies of the event, the retailer and the individual brands enhance the sponsorship participation for everyone.

Keep in mind, too, that some sponsorships can be part barter and part cash. For example, some media partners are willing to give part cash with the balance in trade. Or vendors, such as tent suppliers and other on-site facilities providers, might be willing to barter for 20% of their total billing to the event. Food and beverage people are also viable barter partners.

Other elements to consider? Treat your barter partner as you would any other sponsor. Enter into a contractual relationship with sponsorship benefits and responsibilities clearly spelled out. Maintain the confidentiality of the sponsorship relationship and follow through on all promised benefits. Provide your barter sponsors with the same post-event analysis you would provide to cash sponsors. Demonstrate the value of their sponsorship participation in audience exposure and media impact. Acknowledge them in the same manner as sponsors. The reality is they have helped you either offset a line item expense or enhanced the value of your event with value-added products and/or services. In either case, the relationship has had value. And, you may want to have the same relationship again.

As more event organizers become experienced in barter arrangements, they will enjoy the positive results of these relationships, including decreased expenses and value-added products and services.

Chapter 9 – THE ANNUAL REPORT ... A POWERFUL SALES TOOL

Reading the Annual Report

Annual reports showcase a company to its customers and stockholders. You can get them via the Internet or by calling the Investor Relations department of the company. The introduction of the report sets up the rest of the report by making a good first impression. It often features a letter from the chairman to the stockholders describing the previous year and plans for the future. By reading this section closely, you can generally determine what the company considers important, what is happening that's exciting and what problems the company expects to face. Look for a company overview as well as important information about the company's structure, markets, products and customers.

Finally, just before the financial information, you'll find a more objective explanation of operating results. A word of caution: Companies want to use the introduction to paint as flattering a picture of the company as possible. As you read, look for the following information.

1. **Vision or mission statement** - Mission statements can help galvanize and unify employees for a common goal. Also, if the company makes purchasing decisions with its mission in mind, you need to know what that mission is.

2. **Strategies for achieving the mission** - These plans should tell you a little about the economic constraints of the business environment and describe how the company will use its resources to gain a competitive edge and reach its goals. Most companies list between three and five specific business strategies. Analyze them carefully and decide how your sponsorship offering can make each one more effective.

3. **Principal lines of business** - Many large companies actually comprise several businesses rolled into one. The more you know about the different businesses they're in, the more selling opportunities you may find. Pay close attention to recent acquisitions to find out where the company is headed and what new markets it holds for your sponsorship.

4. **Customers/target market** - Your sponsorship will be much more appealing if it helps the company's customers in a cost-effective, measurable way. Annual reports often illustrate how the company has served its customers. Study these examples to help you understand how the company adds value for its customers.

5. **Challenges and problems** - Focus on any mention of current or future competition, industry or economic trends or how the companys' target market perceives its products and services. Presenting yourself as a problem solver gives your prospect one more good reason to buy.

6. **Measurements of success** - Although some measurements of success are consistent from company to company, individual businesses measure achievement in different ways. Present the benefits of your sponsorship in terms that are meaningful to your

prospects, and they'll recognize the value of what you offer - and that your selling approach is truly customer-oriented.

7. **Sources of competitive advantage** - In some industries, a business gains a competitive edge from being a low-cost producer. In others, it might be more important for a company to develop new products faster or make deliveries promptly. To sell your sponsors on competitive advantage, you'll need to know what your sponsor must do to gain that advantage.

Financial Statements

In this section, pay close attention to the company's income statement. To help you understand what you're reading and what the figures mean remember 1) the numbers acquire meaning only in comparison with a company's past performance and to other companies in the industry, 2) percentages are more important than absolute numbers, and 3) numbers only offer clues as to a company's performance - they tell you the final score, but not how the game was played.

If contemplating your prospect's income statement leaves you wondering where to begin, follow this four-step plan:

1. **Analyze your prospect company's top line or total revenues.** Did sales increase or decrease and why? How did revenue growth compare to industry trends? Was growth attributable more to volume increases or price increases?

2. **Skip down to the bottom line.** Compare profit increases or decreases to revenue increases or decreases. How did their profits compare to their peer group?

3. **Analyze the operating income figures.** Also shown as earnings before interest and taxes, these figures should appear several lines about the net income figure. Operating income numbers are the best measure of how well company managers run the company's day-to-day operations. These figures factor out decisions about company finances and taxes and extraordinary events, where your products will have no impact anyway.

4. **Take a look at gross profit margins.** A company's gross profits are a valuable measure of its effectiveness and ability to add value for its customers. Large revenue increases accompanied by lower gross profit margins, for example, may mean that the company can attract more business only through lower prices.

Since customers and prospects don't come with directions or an owner's manual explaining how to sell to them, why not take advantage of the next best thing? Competitive salespeople need to use all the resources at their disposal, and an annual report provides fast, easy access to valuable customer information.

It's impossible to know much about your prospects and customers. Annual reports are a gold mine of information and serve as a how-to guide for selling to any company that publishes one.

Why Use Annual Reports?

Here are three good reasons to make annual reports part of your selling strategy:

- ♦ **To be more than just a vendor.** Professionals want salespeople to know their business and industry, their sources of competitive advantage, challenges and opportunities - information you can find in many company's annual reports.

- ♦ **To earn the right to an appointment.** You can use the information in an annual report to demonstrate a thorough knowledge of your sponsor's business that will help you get an appointment. The annual report can also familiarize you with the customer-specific jargon, financial measurements and current trends that will help you "speak the language" when you do get an appointment.

- ♦ **To find out how you can help.** Consider a company's annual report the scorecard of its performance. Careful analysis can tell you how you and your sponsorship might be able to enhance that performance - ideas you can then present to your customer in a persuasive presentation.

Chapter 10 – PROPOSAL WRITING/PROPOSAL ASSESSING

Proposals are very individual documents. They are individual to the sponsorship seeking organization; they are individual to the specific corporation to be approached. For sponsorship investments over $1,000 there is no such thing as a generic proposal.

That said, proposals come in all sizes and shapes. Some very successful organizations never send more than a single page the first time they contact a prospect in writing. Others never send out a written proposal of fewer than ten pages.

Most successful proposals, however, do have commonalties.

At the most basic level, there is no excuse for anything less than absolute accuracy in corporate names, addresses, titles and the like. Beyond that, successful proposals are designed to be read quickly or skimmed easily for the key points: what is the event; what does it offer the sponsor in terms of value; what does it cost. If this information is buried, the prospect may not dig. (Remember the one page fact sheet?)

Years ago, sponsorship proposals might have been read by anyone in a corporation from a summer student helping out the CEO's secretary to a junior in accounting. Today, in most corporations, the individual reading sponsorship proposals is a thoroughgoing professional. Smart sponsorship seekers recognize this fact.

Rhetoric about the organization to be sponsored is kept to a minimum. Similarly, a review of the prospect's corporate history and sponsorship profile is not required. (The reader has this information.) The best proposals avoid vague promises. If, for example, increased sales are promised there must be an indication that the proposal writer understands what motivates sales. The same goes for promises to enhance corporate image or to improve community relations.

Sponsorship professionals have cautioned against putting faith in high-priced, over-packaged proposals. These individuals agree that it's the offer that makes the difference. This is not to say that an attention-getting device doesn't have its place, but it should be chosen with care and underpinned with solid business rationale.

Timing

The larger the sponsorship fee, the more highly leveraged the sponsorship is likely to be and the more lead time sponsorship seekers need to allow for corporate decision-making and subsequent development of the sponsorship.

For sponsorships above $10,000 in fee alone, the proposal process should get underway (initial contact made) a minimum of six months in advance of the event. One year in advance is typical for larger investments – even 18 months.

The timing for presentation of the full proposal - a separate consideration - depends on the financial cycle of the corporation (available from annual reports). As a guideline, sponsorship proposals for events of some financial magnitude are submitted a minimum of three to six months before the corporate prospect's fiscal year-end.

Putting both timing requirements together (number of months prior to the event and number of months prior to corporate year-end) can result in a lead-time of eighteen months or more for a significant sponsorship. In this discussion, what constitutes "significant" depends on the corporation, not on the sponsorship seeker.

Proposal assessing

For corporate sponsors, the link between the definitions of corporate objectives -- whether related to sales targets, corporate image, product introduction, community relations, or any other purpose -- and the assessment of any individual proposal, is very direct. In many situations, a given proposal clearly fits or does not fit with corporate objectives. Demographics of event attendees either do or do not match their target. Sampling opportunities either do or do not match requirements. The client hospitality opportunity either is or is not in line with what's required.

The challenge comes when an event offers some of the requirements -- but not others. For example, when an airline sets as a specific corporate objective the exploitation of particular air routes, sponsorships which contribute to the accomplishment of that objective no doubt get special consideration. To continue the example, assume that development of existing Caribbean routes is high on the corporate agenda. Sponsorships of festivals, sports teams, cultural exhibitions, and culinary competitions with a Caribbean focus will be particularly well received and conscientiously evaluated.

But what happens when demographics of event attendees are correct, but media coverage or sheer size of the event is out of line? These are the proposals -- and the occasions -- when the corporation may want to take the lead in shaping the direction and scope of the event behind the proposal. The objectives of the sponsorship seeker and corporation may come into full alignment with the corporate sponsor taking the lead.

Those assessing sponsorship proposals need to be especially aware of the needs of a variety of their internal colleagues, at a variety of levels within the corporation. If a corporation seeks to position itself as a youthful, high-energy organization -- an enormous variety of sponsorship opportunities might well contribute to the image. But thinking must go beyond image to the very specific objectives to be accomplished. Is the youth/energy image important primarily as an appeal to potential shareholders? To the marketplace? To the attraction of new employees?

Sponsorships exist which can contribute to the accomplishment of the whole spectrum of goals. The challenge to those assessing sponsorship proposals is to match corporate objectives to the benefits available from the sponsorship seeker.

Related thinking

Sponsorship? Charitable contribution? Corporate philanthropy? Does it matter what we call it?

Of course it does ... enormously.

All those who seek funding had best know which corporate pocket they're applying to. The request for a donation is vastly different from the proposal for a sponsorship relationship. The contact point is different; the goals are different; the language is different.

It matters, too, on the corporate side because of the widely differing goals of the donations committee, for example, and the brand management team. The opportunity for leverage is the single largest loss that comes from corporate confusion about the differences between sponsorship and charity.

Are there hybrids?

Of course there are, especially where large sums or complex funding requirements are involved. Or where a corporation continues under the leadership of a founding entrepreneur who is likely to make personal decisions on both sponsorships and charitable contributions.

The chart on the following page provides a quick overview of the differences between sponsorship and charitable contributions.

Following is a chart that compares sponsorship and charitable contributions.

	Sponsorship	Charitable Contribution
Publicity	Highly public	Usually little widespread fanfare
Source	Typically from marketing, advertising or communications budgets	From charitable donations or philanthropy budgets
Accounting	Written off as a full business expense, like promotional printing expenses or media from placement expenses	Write-off is limited to 75% of net income. As a result, accounting/tax considerations are less likely to influence the way a corporation designates funding of a not-for-profit organization
Objectives	To sell more products/services; to increase positive awareness in markets and among distant stakeholders (customers, potential customers, geographic community); etc.	To be a good corporate citizen; to enhance the corporate image with closest stakeholders (employees, shareholders, suppliers); to help the non-profit survive
Partner/recipient	Events; teams, arts or cultural organizations; projects; programs. A non-profit is sometimes associated with the undertaking	Larger donations are typically cause-related (education, health, diseases, environmental, disasters), but can also be cultural, artistic or sports related. At times funding is specifically designated for a project or programs; other times it is provided for operating budgets
Where most funding goes	Sports get the lion's share of sponsorship dollars...around 65%	Education, social services, and the health sector get 75% of charitable donations

31

Chapter 11 – HOW TO PRICE YOUR EVENT COMPONENTS

Where do you start on determining a fair market value for your sponsorship offering? As you know from the 12 steps to sponsorship success, you start by taking inventory … what do you have to sell … which could include banners, collateral material such as posters/flyers/brochures, hospitality opportunities, on-site participation and exposure, tickets, etc., etc., etc.

Once you have taken your inventory – what you have to sell – and have determined the quantity (100,000 flyers, 20,000 tickets, etc.), you can begin to attach value to these components. Here are some basic "rules of thumb" to use:

- Logo/name in event ads   10% of total value (rate card)
- Radio/full advertising   rate card/%-age of time
- TV   rate card/%-age of time
- VIP passes, parking, tickets   face value
- Booth/display area   rate card
- Logo on t-shirts, merchandise $20 CPM
- Sampling opportunity $150 CPM
- Mailing list $65 CPM
- PA announcements $10 CPM
- Value of PR $10 CPM
- Billboards $1.50 CPM*
- Internet $1.50 CPM
- Table Tents $75 CPM
- Flyers $50 CPM
- Posters $35 CPM
- Payroll stuffers $75 CPM
- On-site banners $100 CPM

*get your traffic count from your local Department of Transportation.

Now, you have the basic values. Next, you multiply the quantities by the values and you know the total valuation of your offering. However, you're not done yet!

Who gets what sponsorship benefits? Title sponsor gets everything since they are paying for title value, category exclusivity and are partnering with you for perceived ownership. How you allocate benefits to the other sponsors --- supporting, participating, whatever --- is up to you. It is wise to have a basic idea of benefits allocation prior to contacting your sponsors but be prepared to modify/change your sponsorship offerings based on the wants and needs of your potential sponsors. By being flexible in your offerings you are more likely to be successful in your sponsorship sales. As always, use your common sense and good judgment when negotiating with your sponsors. (See Appendix E for chart to be used in preparing pricing components of your sponsorship offering.)

Chapter 12 - WITHOUT MEDIA, YOUR SPONSORSHIP PACKAGE LACKS STRENGTH

How do you get media involved in your event? The same way you would any other sponsor. Sounds simple doesn't it.

To start, you should have your sponsorship components already established and in place. For example, you should know what benefits are associated with each level of sponsorship including signage, hospitality, collateral material, on-site exposure, contests, promotions, etc. In addition, you should have determined your pricing and value, keeping in mind that you always want to give double value for the investment. (One of your selling strategies is to let your potential sponsors know, and understand, that if each component were purchased individually, it would cost twice as much as the investment you are asking them to make.)

Once you have determined the various sponsorship levels and the components included in these offerings, you can approach your media about participating as a sponsor. And, you approach them in a positive manner: you have something to offer them ... you don't have to be apologetic for your offerings and the marketing opportunities and exposure offered by your particular event.

Who to Approach

When selecting media sponsors, you follow the same guidelines as selecting your other sponsorship partners. Is this the right fit? Does your event have the right demographics, psychographics, geographic location, attendance, etc. that match the needs of the sponsor? Does your event fit into that medium's marketing strategy? Will it attract more listeners, viewers or readers? For example, if you have an event that attracts Generation Xers, you certainly wouldn't select the New York Times; or, if you have a family event, you wouldn't select an alternative music or heavy metal radio station. Be as selective in determining your media partners as you are with your other sponsors.

Where to Start

The most logical person to start with in radio or TV is the General Manager (GM); in newspapers or magazines it would be the Publisher or Senior Editor. As overall management, they can quickly comprehend the value of being associated with your event, the impact on the community, the importance to them of reaching new readers/viewers/listeners (depending on whether you are talking to them about newspaper or magazine sponsorship, television or radio sponsorship), and how that sponsorship can enhance their exposure in the community.

The next best contact person is the Sales Manager or, following that, the Promotions Manager. If meeting with the latter, see if you can get the GM, Publisher or President to sit in on your presentation. This way you won't have to wait for the Promotions Manager to present the materials to someone else to make the decision.

How to Present the Material

As with other sponsors, keep their goals and objectives in mind. Take time to find out as much as you can about the radio or TV station, newspaper or magazine, before the meeting so you can talk to them knowledgeably. Request a media kit ... read the material. Know the rankings for the radio and TV stations; know the circulation of the magazines and newspapers you are approaching and how that circulation compares to their competition. In short, DO YOUR HOMEWORK!

Present your sponsorship materials as you would for any other sponsor. Explain the investment and what the value of that investment is in event benefits. Although you probably will end up with a straight trade agreement, you could start your negotiation asking for money and negotiating your way down. You might be surprised; there have been many media deals that have included not only the media exposure but some cash investment as well. Keep in mind that your goal is to have sufficient media that can be included in your sponsorship offerings that will have value to your other sponsors.

Negotiation

When negotiating for the media, do so at rate card prices. Don't try to get them to give you a "special deal". If they do, you will have to reciprocate. You want to end up with sufficient radio and TV spots, plus newspaper and magazine advertising, to properly promote your event and offer bonus media exposure to your sponsors. If you are a non-profit, you have a negotiating "edge" because the media feel a responsibility to provide coverage to not-for-profit organizations.

In addition to commercials and advertising coverage, you want to negotiate for other media coverage: radio remotes, newscast coverage, feature stories, etc. And, although advertising and editorial don't mix, you can usually negotiate a multi-component contract that is win/win for both sides.

Closing the Deal

As with your other sponsors, draw up a contract with all the sponsorship rights and benefits clearly spelled out. Provide them with updates on what is happening, involve them in the production and planning process, keep them involved during the entire event, and provide them with a post-event report...same strategy as your other sponsors. In turn, you will want from them, after the event, an audited traffic summary (radio/TV) and tear sheets (print). The more documentation that each of you provides the other, the more professional the arrangement. And, the more likely they are to renew year after year after year.

Chapter 13 – WHAT TELEVISION LOOKS FOR IN A SPONSORSHIP PARTNERSHIP

Event planners often start their search for sponsors with a television partner. This is an important first step because of the guaranteed publicity muscle of television. The added value of television exposure is a key marketing tool in attracting top corporate sponsors. Television stations receive hundreds of requests to sponsor events each year, everything from pie eating contests at county fairs to huge expos that attract hundreds of thousands of business professionals. Audience size and demographics are important, but they are not the sole criteria a television station will use in deciding if they will sponsor an event. Here are some guidelines television uses when evaluating sponsorships:

- It must be consistent with who the station is and who they want to be.
- Is it consistent with their branding?
- Does it meet the needs of the community?
- It must increase awareness of the station, programming and talent.
- It must help differentiate them from their competition.
- Does the event have revenue-generating opportunities?
- What is the track record of the event organizers?
- Does it provide a database opportunity?
- What is the date of the event? (The stations like to plan one year in advance)
- Judgments are based on the station's resources, people and inventory.

It's imperative to reach an agreement at the onset with event organizers on the responsibilities of each partner and determine exactly what each partner will bring to the table. Just as imperative is establishing a time line for the completion of tasks. Missed deadlines are often the first sign that a partner is falling behind or unable to handle a task.

It's also very important for the organizer and partners to create an event strategy to properly analyze the value of the sponsorship, share database information and maintain a good relationship with key contacts.

Here are some things to look for from the event team:

- Good communications;
- Good relationships with key contacts;
- Honest evaluation of the event;
- A time line;
- Clear understanding of responsibilities; and,

35

- Added opportunities for exposure for the television station.

As an event sponsor, TV looks for high recognition of their sponsorship. It's great to be identified on press releases, signage, flyers, entry forms and posters, but it loses its value if the station is lost in a "sea of logos".

Everyone wants an event organizer who understands his or her business. They become valuable partners. It's important to understand the value of a station's on-air commitment of time. The on-air time is money and, through sponsorship, tries to return that value through receiving event benefits.

Chapter 14 – WHAT RADIO WANTS IN A SPONSORSHIP

Not only are sponsors being bombarded with more sponsorship opportunities, so, too, are radio stations. And, with the proliferation of sponsorship opportunities, how can you differentiate yours from the competition? If you take time to understand what your radio partner wants, and expects, from the sponsorship relationship, you will be more successful is having them participate in your event.

Your radio sponsor is one of the first partnerships you establish when soliciting sponsorships since you need their participation to enhance the value of your sponsorship package. Any sponsorship over $10,000 should have a radio, as well as television and print, component to enhance the sponsorship package and give greater value to your other sponsors.

Here are some suggested guidelines for establishing your radio partnership:

1. Is my event audience compatible with the radio station's audience? Are the demographics and psychographics similar?

2. When is the event being held? Does it clash with something already committed by the station?

3. Am I giving them enough lead-time? (Hint: Plan a year in advance!).

4. Are you offering the station revenue-generating opportunities? (Cross promotions, a sponsorship package to use as an enhancement for a reluctant advertiser, a sponsor buying additional air time, NTR – non traditional revenue, etc.).

5. Does your event help the station differentiate themselves from their competition?

6. Do you have a cause related marketing tie in? Is there a conflict with the station's own cause(s)?

7. Will the station receive marketing value comparable to the airtime value?

8. How can they enhance their participation? (On-site exposure, remotes, parade participation, announcer at awards presentation, etc.).

9. Does it meet the needs of our community?

They will also want to know your track record, who you have worked with in the past, and the results of that relationship. And, as with any sponsor, you will want to spell out, in a contract, what the expectations are from both parties. This means itemizing what you are providing, as the event organizer, such as banners, signage, on-site booth space, etc. In turn, they should spell out how much air time you will receive, value of remote (if included in the sponsorship), and other marketing opportunities being provided as part of *their* sponsorship contribution.

You also must establish a clearly defined time line for the completion of tasks. Missed deadlines are often the first sign that a partner is falling behind or unable to handle a task.

It's also very important for the organizer and partners to create a post event summary to properly analyze the value of the sponsorship, share database information and maintain a good relationship with key contacts.

Here are some of the things a radio station looks for from an event team:

- Good communications;
- Good relationships with key contacts;
- Honest evaluation of the event;
- A time line;
- Clear understanding of responsibilities; and,
- Added opportunities for exposure for the radio station.

Remember, with radio, airtime is money. You have to demonstrate that the radio station will receive true value for their involvement and be able to validate it upon completion of the event. In addition to providing them with a post-event report and evaluation, your contract should spell out the post-event valuation you will receive from your radio partner including when spots ran, how often they ran, and the market value of those air times. (Does this sound familiar? It's what TV wants as well. See previous chapter.)

Chapter 15 – WHY A RETAIL PARTNER

In many instances you have been told that it helps to have a retail partner involved to increase the success of a consumer product sponsorship. OK ...what does that mean?

Many of you already know how to work with the media by getting them involved, allowing them to use their sponsorship as a value-added "pull through" for their advertisers and potential advertisers. It works in much the same way with the retail partner.

What does a retail outlet have that is valuable to you and your event? Customers, extensive media advertising, and high visibility through in-store display space. And, what do you have that is valuable to the retailer? Attendance (translate that to mean customers), extensive media exposure, and high visibility. You have a match!

In the "chicken/egg" dilemma, do you approach the retailer first and then get the consumer products or vice versa? It makes no difference; however, I think it is easier if you get the retailer on board first and then solicit the consumer products that are carried by that retailer.

Retail outlets can be supermarkets, drugstores, department stores, quick service restaurants (QSR's), gas stations, sporting goods stores, delicatessens/mini-markets ... any store that carries a wide range of products and has customers and display space is a good retail partner. The exact one depends on your event and the appropriateness of the fit. For example, I don't believe the Great Five Boro Bike Tour (a 42 mile bicycle tour through the five boroughs of Manhattan) would be a good partner for a gasoline station; however a health food store, supermarket or drugstore would be a good fit.

Once you have selected the retail outlet, approach them the same way you would any other sponsor with the understanding that you may not get as large a cash sponsorship as you might want but will get valuable barter components that will enhance your event's visibility and exposure. Ask them who they would like to include in their sponsorship. They may have a specific product (or products) that could benefit from the sampling or on-site exposure offered by your event.

Be familiar with your retail partner's advertising efforts. Do they have in-store audio announcements? Can you have an aisle display or end-cap visibility? Do they have advertising on the back of their register tapes? Can you be included? If a supermarket, can you be on the bags? Can you include other sponsors on the print material? Request inclusion in their weekly advertising, flyers and circulars. Can you have on-site visibility through posters and banners? Will they accept bag stuffers? Will they work with you on brand-specific promotions and strategies if those brands are in their stores? Take a close look at *their* inventory, just as they have done with yours, and determine how much of it has value to your event and event sponsors.

Then, solicit specific brands for sponsorship. You have a guaranteed relationship with a retail outlet, you have the power of your event, and you have your media relationships in place. This is a powerful combination to entice sponsors to your event.

Caution: This doesn't happen overnight. Allow a minimum of six months (preferably a year) to develop these cross-marketing tie-ins. This benefits your retail outlet, your brand sponsors and your event. Another win-win situation!

Chapter 16 – PARTNERING WITH YOUR LOCAL CABLE COMPANY

When calling on cable for sponsorship, think about who the appropriate person is within the cable company that will be most interested in the sponsorship relationship. In all probability, it will be the community affairs director or government relations director. And, the most logical cable company to approach is the one with the franchise in the community where your event is being held. That company has a vested interest in the community, is interested in becoming involved in local events as part of their charter and know that their participation is part of their good will outreach to the community. Lastly, it just makes good business sense.

Just as you take inventory of what you have to sell that's of value to your sponsors, understand that the cable company has inventory that will benefit your event. In addition to the obvious benefit of air time, consider the following other assets available through your local cable company:

1. Statement stuffers;
2. Invoice "promotions";
3. Community bulletin board;
4. "Crawlers" across the weather channel;
5. Internet hyperlink/exposure;
6. Event promotion through on-site production/broadcasting;
7. Cable TV guide;
8. Access to cable talent;
9. Costume characters;
10. Celebrity appearances;
11. Cross-promotion with existing cable advertisers.

This is just a partial list. Certainly when negotiating with your local cable provider find out how their assets and inventory have value to you and vice versa. Be willing to do some of your sponsorship on a barter basis. For example, if your title sponsorship is $25,000 and they can offset $10,000 in line items in your budget, through barter, bringing their cash investment to only $15,000, give it consideration. Remember, you are asking for sponsorship dollars to offset the cost of running your event; if the cable sponsor can offset some of those costs through barter, it's the same as cash!

Take time to investigate how you can partner with your cable provider. The time will be wisely invested and the payback, for both of you, will be great!

Chapter 17 – BILLBOARDS AS PART OF YOUR SPONSORSHIP PROGRAM

One of the more neglected sponsorship components is billboards. As with any of the other media, these are viable barter partners. However, before you approach them for sponsorship, consider what their wants and needs are so you can provide a valuable benefit to them through sponsorship of your event.

According to the Outdoor Advertising Association of America (OAAA), billboards and posters are two of the most cost-effective ways of reaching consumers. The billboard, the most commonly used form of outdoor advertising, comes in two standard forms: the 30-sheet poster and the bulletin.

The 30-Sheet Poster

These are lithographed or silk-screened by a printer and shipped to an outdoor advertising company. They are then prepasted and applied in sections to the poster panel's face on location. Standard 30-sheet posters measure approximately 12 feet high by 24 feet wide. The majority of 30-sheet posters are done on rotation, which means that each month the advertiser changes locations. Each time a location is changed a new poster is affixed to the billboard.

The Bulletin

These can be hand-painted in an outdoor company's studio and erected in sections on location, painted directly on the board at the location, or produced by computer and mounted at the location. Most measure 14 feet high by 48 feet wide. The majority of painted bulletins in the United States are permanent boards at extremely high traffic locations, which remain up for at least six months.

Other Types of Outdoor Advertising

In addition to the 30-sheet poster and the bulletin, the following are other types of outdoor advertising :

- 8-sheet poster or junior panels;
- Transit interiors/exteriors;
- Painted walls;
- Telephone kiosks;
- Truck displays;
- Taxi tops;
- Transit/rail platforms;
- Airport/bus terminal displays;
- Transit clock platforms;

- Bus shelter displays;
- Shopping mall displays;
- In-store displays.

Conclusion

In recent years, more and more advertisers have taken advantage of outdoor advertising because of its relative cost efficiency. Billboards are permitted in all states except Maine, Vermont, Hawaii and Alaska.

The cost of an outdoor ad will largely depend upon location. Unlike print advertising, which charges a space rate, billboard advertising sells by "showings". There are three types of showings: 100, 50 and 35. A 50 showing, for example, is seen approximately 14 times a month by approximately 90% of the area's population. The billboard company can help you select the location(s) that attracts the particular demographic population you are trying to reach. When pitching a billboard company for sponsorship, keep in mind that tickets and other hospitality opportunities are important to them for entertaining and selling to their own clients.

Chapter 18 – PARTNERING WITH YOUR LOCAL NEWSPAPER (a case history)

Knight-Ridder Inc. (KR) is an international communications company with daily newspapers across America. Their event marketing initiative began in 1993 as part of a comprehensive new strategy to augment traditional newspaper revenues, increase public awareness of the papers, and enhance relationships with current and future advertisers.

After carefully researching their markets, they determined that certain consumer show formats--women's shows, home shows, boat/RV/auto shows, and outdoor/lifestyle/shows--offered unique marketing opportunities for many of their newspaper advertisers and could also be useful events for their readers. They entered the consumer show business to give their advertisers a new target marketing tool and to offer their readers another forum to test, sample and buy products and services. Their newspapers are now involved in many consumer shows a year.

They recognized early on that independent show producers have the staff and expertise their papers lacked. Reputation is vitally important to their newspapers--they don't want to fail in the public eye. Long after a show has closed, they remain in the community, maintaining relationships with advertisers and building trust among readers. They initially chose to partner with two organization, Southern Shows and Southex exhibitions, because they have impeccable reputations, each with a long history of successful events, and they meshed well with KR in their target markets.

Through these alliances, KR has been able to create successful new events and drive up attendance at existing shows; in turn, these events have helped generate new advertising revenue, incrementally increase circulation and enhance the visibility of their newspapers in the communities they served.

What newspapers bring to the table

Because they have established relationships with their local advertisers, they have access to community leaders who may be willing to work with them in promoting a new event. They invite their clients to sponsor a stage, promote a giveaway or host a major celebrity for the event. The possibilities are limited only by the imagination. Event managers at KR papers work closely with the show managers to develop marketing strategies and sales proposals for local and national companies. They help to promote space and sponsorship sales and create special attendance promotions with advertisers.

For the Miami Home Show, which they produced with Southex, they created an advertising and promotion package for a local developer, who gave away a beachfront condo. They received 200,000 entries in the contest and attracted more than 50,000 people to the nine-day event. For other events, they designated a major supermarket chain as the exclusive ticket outlet and worked with the chain to create massive in-store promotions—the advertisers benefited from the increased traffic in their stores, the newspapers gained visibility and the show's attendance climbed.

It is this type of intensive local promotion that newspapers make possible. The shows also get a guaranteed advertising buy at a special rate. In turn, KR receives a percentage share in the show revenues.

What show producers have to offer

In today's hotly competitive environment, show producers can offer newspapers strong opportunities to generate incremental revenue and gain exposure for advertisers through high-profile promotions and sponsorships. These factors become increasingly important in larger markets, but they can be the basis for relationships in small-to-medium markets as well. That's why newspapers continue to look for alliance and joint venture opportunities.

When an independent show organizer approaches a newspaper about co-producing an event, there are several elements that can make a deal attractive:

- A unique concept that is new in the market, fills a niche or rides an emerging trend--advanced technology.

- A history of producing successful events--the producer has a solid reputation.

- A well-developed plan for launching the show, with a clearly defined role for the newspaper--a special advertising section alone doesn't always make it a worthwhile deal.

- Specific strategies for selling sponsorships, generating advertising and promoting circulation.

- Realistic revenue and expense projections, with a bottom-line estimate of what the newspaper's participation means to them.

Competitors or partners?

Newspapers are always looking for new event niches that will help them better serve their advertisers and readers. Marketing managers at papers want to know what's going to set them apart from their competitors, and how a show can enhance their relations with key advertisers or open doors to potential new advertisers. When the newspaper becomes a partner with the show producer--and it takes time and trust to make these relationships grow--each partner reaps rewards and the community as a whole gets a first-class event.

45

Chapter 19 – HOSPITALITY: THE SILENT BENEFIT

One of the most common components of sponsorship is hospitality. And, hospitality programs come in all sizes ... large or small, expensive or inexpensive, formal or informal. How it fits into the framework of sponsorship depends upon the needs of the *sponsors*, not the event. A hospitality component can be included for entertaining customers, rewarding or entertaining employees, hosting trade partners, and soliciting new customers, to name just a few.

Looking at the hospitality options more closely, you need to discuss the hospitality opportunities with the sponsor. If entertaining customers, how many people will be involved? What are your responsibilities? Their responsibilities? Be as detailed as possible and incorporate those details in your contract.

If this is an employee program, will it be used as a family event, a reward for outstanding sales performance or as an adjunct to their existing human resources program (i.e. company picnic, holiday celebration, etc.)? Again, clearly understand their needs so the proper space can be allocated, define each other's responsibilities, and include these details in the contract.

An important use of hospitality is in trade relationships. For example, a major bottler may want to invite his/her suppliers to your event or use your event to showcase their products to potential business customers. As with all your sponsorship sales efforts, you can help your sponsors determine their best use of the hospitality component by asking questions that demonstrate your knowledge of their business and helping them formulate the hospitality component.

For the hospitality component of sponsorship you need to do just as much planning as you would for the actual event itself. That means, establish a budget, be sensitive to the needs of the sponsors, be prepared to handle everything or nothing, and be highly detailed in all elements of the hospitality component (just like the other components!). Also, keep in mind that there is usually an additional fee for the hospitality element (tent, caterers, flowers, tables, chairs, etc.) that is over and above the sponsorship investment.

To effectively implement the hospitality segment of a sponsorship, you need a detailed hospitality plan...a checklist, detailed site layout, contingency plans (in case something goes wrong), a formal walk through, and an informed staff ... all which will facilitate a smooth (and successful) hospitality component to your sponsorship program.

Chapter 20 – UNDERSTANDING THE SPONSOR'S REVIEW PROCESS (from the sponsor's point-of-view)

When selling sponsorships, it's important to understand what corporations use to determine their participation. The following is a list of selection criteria used by corporations:

1. Can the company afford to fulfill the obligation? The sponsorship fee is just the starting point. Count on doubling it to give yourself an adequate total event budget.

2. Is the event or organization compatible with the company's values and mission statement?

3. Does the event reach our target audience?

4. Is there enough time before the event to maximize our use of the sponsorship?

5. Are the event organizers experienced and professional?

6. Is the event newsworthy enough to provide us with opportunities for publicity?

7. Will the event be televised?

8. Will the sales force support the event and use it to leverage sales?

9. Does the event give us the chance to develop new contacts and develop new business opportunities?

10. Can we live with this event on a long-term basis while its value builds?

11. Is there an opportunity for employee goodwill and teamwork? Employee involvement can also contribute to the success of the event.

12. Is the event compatible with the "personality" of our products?

13. Can we shrink the cash outlay for the company and enhance the marketing appeal of the event by trading off products and in-kind services?

14. Will management support the event?

If you've answered yes to all the previous questions, the likelihood of management support of the sponsorship is fairly high.

During an era in which corporate investment in traditional forms of mass communications has stagnated, spending on sponsorships continues to grow. In 2005, it is estimated that sponsorship spending alone will exceed $11 billion.

Now, a drive to maximize the value of sponsorships is catching up with the spending explosion. In the early 1980s, many corporate and firm practitioners were reluctant to acknowledge any significant value in sponsorships. However, that changed dramatically in the 1990s as any peek at the ubiquitous corporate logos on display at major sporting or cultural events today confirms. The 2000's now call for strong measurement and accountability as well as offering other partnership opportunities.

Following are some of the key points that may help guide you in refining your own criteria. This mindset is useful for corporate and communications professionals considering sponsorships, as well as for those involved in pitching sponsorships to prospects.

Evaluation

As with any public relations program, an evaluation completes the loop with a check to see if the original objectives were fulfilled. Some of the key questions to ask include:

- Did the event grow?
- Did the organizers deliver on their promises?
- Were TV ratings as expected?
- Did retailers support the effort?
- Did the event prove newsworthy?
- Did top management get involved?
- Did sales grow?
- Did the sponsor make new contacts and solidify new contracts?
- Did the sponsor leave an impression of their company that is consistent with their unifying theme and mission?
- Did the business units indicate an interest in investing again?

Understanding a sponsor's pre-event selection criteria and post-event evaluation will enhance your sponsorship sales ability.

Chapter 21 – USING SPONSORSHIP FOR BUSINESS-TO-BUSINESS PURPOSES

So much of sponsorship is about marketing to the general public, i.e. consumers. However, there is a whole business-to-business sponsorship area that needs to be explored.

Here are nine key questions that sponsors should use for evaluating a sponsorship offering designated specifically to help them with their business-to-business marketing.

1. Why are they doing this?

Sponsors should first determine why they are getting involved in this sponsorship. For example, here are some reasons for involvement:

- Forge new links with opinion leaders;
- Reward top salespeople;
- Create employee incentives;
- Attract new customers;
- Thank old customers;
- Demonstrate category leadership;
- Open new channels of distribution;
- Offer hospitality opportunities ...employees, customers, dealers.

By understanding their reasons for participation, you can present an appropriate sponsorship to meet their needs.

2. Does the property enhance/reinforce the company's image and leadership among their customers?

If they are the industry leader, and want to maintain that position, they will want a sponsorship that supports that strategy. Conversely, if they aren't the leader, but want to be, they might want to get involved in a sponsorship that would help them achieve the leadership position.

3. Does the property create additional customer loyalty?

Assuming the investment is strictly for a business-to-business marketing strategy, if the sponsorship investment also reaches consumers there is additional value to the participation.

4. Are there seasonal implications?

Simply, don't ask accountants to get involved in sponsorships that would occur during the first quarter of the year when they are burdened with preparing tax returns! Know your sponsors' industries, be sensitive to *their* needs, and respond accordingly.

5. What are the opportunities?

The complete package should include tickets, media and hospitality. Make sure, again, you address the needs of the sponsor, setting aside your needs as the promoter. Understand the sponsor's business so you can present a package of benefits that has value.

6. What is my exposure?

Sponsors are interested in having "space", not being involved in too much clutter. They also don't want to see their competitors there so category/product exclusivity is valuable to them.

7. What is the payback?

What can the sponsor expect from their involvement? Again, understanding the sponsor's business will help you be more effective in determining sponsorship benefits and components that will help the sponsor achieve his/her objective.

8. What is the perceived value to the sponsor's clients?

In business-to-business marketing there are hundreds of thousands of options available from the simple sponsorship of a golf foursome to an elaborate title sponsorship of a major event. How the sponsor's clients perceive the involvement is important in determining the value of the sponsorship to the sponsoring organization.

9. Can the involvement be expanded to include employees?

Often, a business-to-business sponsorship can be used to enhance current business relationships, whether with past, present or future customers. For example, Canada Dry used a recent sponsorship at the Garden State Arts Center strictly for enhancing their trade relationships. Special pre-event dinners were held for the trade with priority parking passes and priority seating for the attendees as part of the benefits of sponsorship.

In addition, these business-to-business sponsorships can involve employees as well. The sponsorship can be used to reward outstanding employees, be an opportunity to involve all employees as a way of saying "thanks", or be used as an incentive for salespeople. Several years ago, Household Finance Corporation sponsored a series of offshore races in their key markets for the sole purpose of employee relations. HFC families were invited to the events, large hospitality tents were set up with food and beverage, and the entire family was involved.

Conclusion

Then, you follow the same rules as you would with any other sponsorship. Have the sponsor involved early in the process and make sure there is total corporate involvement. Have a contract that clearly defines benefits and obligations on both sides with accountability and checks and balances. Make sure the company knows their objectives and make sure you know yours!

50

Chapter 22 – HOW TO GET THE MOST VALUE FROM YOUR SPORTS SPONSORSHIP (from the sponsor's point-of-view)

Your organization has just decided to sponsor a professional sporting event. Whether it's golf, tennis, road races or soccer, there are certain basics to keep in mind to maximize your return on your investment.

Sports Sponsorships Reach a Variety of Audiences

Used properly, the sports sponsorship can have a very positive effect on your customers, the trade, and on your employees. Sports sponsorship builds cohesiveness and a sense of pride and teamwork into an organization. Its value can even extend to relationships with community leaders, government, and news media.

When it comes to sports sponsorship, media exposure is a major factor motivating large organizations. Yet media exposure should not be the sole motivating factor. Other factors? Reaching key customers and prospects.

The following points can maximize the value of a sports sponsorship:

1. Make sure the event is integrated into your organization's overall marketing plan. There is no point in spending money and time to support an event if it does not help you achieve a marketing objective or a behavioral goal. Objectives must be clear and realistic.

2. Don't use words like "position", "promote", and "publicize" for your objectives. Do use such words as "gain", "grow", or "increase". If providing exposure and building awareness are the only aims you can identify, you may have difficulty sustaining corporate approval for your programs.

3. Don't neglect research. Find out as much as possible about the demographics and psychographics of your target audience. How often do they attend or participate in a particular sport? What are their buying habits? Research will help forge a meaningful link between sponsorships and objectives. Get information on your product, the market, and your customers. How do you get this information? Surveys, studies, focus groups, media coverage -- these are all valuable resources.

4. What's your long-term strategy? Like a well-tended garden, a thoughtfully designed sponsorship can bring you more substantial benefits as time goes on. Your investment today is for the future. One-time-only events may give your organization a welcome spurt of recognition, but the effects will not be long-lived without continuity. It takes time to establish partnerships with co-sponsors and develop effective cross-promotions.

5. Is the program compatible with your image? Think about your target audience. Does the event reach them? Does it entertain in good taste? Does it portray you as a good corporate citizen? Will the community or charity reap benefit from the event? Public service alone provides a good return.

6. Leverage your investment. Your ultimate goal is to achieve the broadest return possible. It is a costly mistake to affix your name to an event without calculating how you will promote, merchandise, advertise, build and reinforce the organization.

7. Include the trade and salespeople. Look at ways to generate added trade and sales force support and enthusiasm. Advise the sales staff to use the event as a tool. Chances are, most of your sales force participates in or follows the event, so build in opportunities for them to be involved. It is also a good idea to directly involve employees from other departments.

8. Create innovative pre-event activities. These can generate general publicity. For example, schedule a "media day" three to four weeks ahead of the event. Develop participatory activities for the press in addition to the usual news briefing. For example, if the upcoming event is a golf tournament, arrange for the media to play golf with the top pros or the defending champion.

9. Identify "key" print and broadcast reporters. Plan well in advance of your event. Find out who will be assigned to cover the event and what aspects they will cover, e.g. features or play-by-play. This is particularly important at the major dailies, which may have more than one reporter who covers a particular sport or event. Stay in touch with them and offer news and feature updates as you get closer to the event.

10. Use the sanctioning body or sport's national association (PGA, USTA, etc.) as an information resource. They can provide helpful and current information to the news media.

11. Last, but certainly not least, measurement. Tabulate the results by looking at:

- **Media coverage**, i.e., clippings. (By the way, in a title sponsorship, negotiate to have your company/product name in the name of the event, e.g. the Buick Open, the Volvo Tennis Classic, etc.)

- **Pre- and post-sponsorship surveys.** What was the amount of sponsor and/or product recall? Did attitudes change?

- **Relationships**. Did sponsorship bring you closer to your employees? The media? Members of the community? Customers?

- **Actual responses delivered**. Were any leads generated? Did sales increase? Did you achieve any behavioral objectives?

Be sure to allocate enough time in total people-hours to accomplish objectives. Build in at least 20% more time than you think it will take to do the job. Sports events are terrific opportunities to support your organization's goals, involve your employees, achieve corporate marketing objectives and.. have fun at the same time!

Chapter 23 – MAKE YOUR SPONSORSHIP A "WIN-WIN" BY ASKING THE RIGHT QUESTIONS (from the sponsor's point-of-view)

The next time you read a newspaper or magazine article about a sport or special event, see if there is any mention of the participating sponsor's name. If so, the sponsor has just scored a publicity "coup" that cannot be easily measured in dollars. The public relations impact is so much stronger than the same amount of coverage in advertising space that there is no comparison. More and more companies are realizing that sponsorship, carefully planned and skillfully executed, can be a win-win situation -- a boon for both the sponsors and the event. Poorly thought out, sponsorship can be a costly mistake.

Each year, more sports and special events take place, creating a greater number of sponsorship opportunities for a diversity of products and services. However, not all of these opportunities are for all sponsors. To get the most from sponsorship, make sure that both sponsor and event organizers' needs and expectations are being met.

Here are some questions to ask when deciding whether an event is right for you.

1. Who is attracted to the event, in terms of both spectators and participants?

Are these the people I am trying to reach through my marketing efforts or will my message be misdirected?

2. Who are the other sponsors?

Am I in good company? Do I have too much company? One of the appeals of event sponsorship is that it helps corporations avoid the "ad clutter" of other media. If there are too many sponsors, your name could be lost.

3. What are the sponsorship benefits?

Am I included in the press kits? Do I participate in all the media events? What on-site recognition/acknowledgment -- signage, introductions, opportunities for product demonstration -- will I have? What is my visibility to those who are attending? To those who are watching on TV?

4. What is the goal of my sponsorship, and do the answers to the previous questions indicate that I will reach it?

The goal is not always a direct sell of product or service. Firms may use special event involvement to provide sales incentives; to enhance dealer and employee loyalty by inviting them to events; to provide an opportunity for product demonstration; for goodwill, giving current customers the opportunity to rub shoulders with the top brass; and/or to build a company's image.

5. Will I get my money's worth?

What is the history of the event? How have other sponsors fared? If this is a first-time event, what bonus breaks are being offered as an inducement to participate? What is its potential longevity? Do I have right of first refusal for upcoming years?

Results -- particularly those geared to image enhancement -- may be difficult to quantify. Some companies do ask their sales forces to track sales before and after, and indicate if those figures showed a positive response. Others hire a tracking service, which measures exposure time and offers advice on such topics as how to increase logo visibility.

In the final analysis, each sponsor must answer the question, "Is it worth it?" based on its own investment, goals and results. As a sponsor, you want to reach your markets at the attendees lifestyle level, making sure the audience is receptive and qualified to receive your message. You want to be assured of maximum coverage. And you want to know that your involvement is long-term, to ensure maximum benefit.

Chapter 24 – SPONSOR SELECTION CRITERIA

Most people, prior to a job interview, take the time to learn as much as possible about the company where they are interviewing. Yet, it's astonishing that most of the property representatives that call on either sponsors or agency people looking for a sponsor speak about how "perfect" XYZ company would be for their property, without even the basic understanding of what XYZ company is and what it is trying to accomplish!

For those few who do take the time to learn about prospective sponsors' needs, the upside is enormous. They can then tailor a proposal accordingly and steer the decision-maker in the desired direction. Having the knowledge of the prospect and its needs is always the most important element in any property solicitation.

Although each prospective sponsor has different and specific objectives, there will also be some basic/general criteria that need to be used to assess the property's potential value as a partner. Any variances that do exist do so with respect to the weight each client gives each of these criteria.

Following are 15 criteria above and beyond the basic demographic and reach statistics that are looked at when assessing a property's value (in no specific order of importance, as each client has different objectives).

1. Does the property enhance/reinforce the company's image and product leadership among consumers? Remember, image is everything. It doesn't matter how many people attend an event if the event's image isn't compatible with the image/positioning of the prospective sponsor.

2. Does the property create a high level of loyalty/affinity between fans and sponsors? Again, numbers of fans/attendees are less important than the level of intensity of their loyalty. This is why NASCAR is so popular. Its passionate fans really care that the sport's sponsors are helping to support their sport while other properties may not be able to make the same claim

3. What are the seasonal implications of the sport/event, and are they in alignment with the brands? Many companies focus their marketing efforts against certain timeframes. If you're looking for a financial services company, a February event, prior to the April 15 tax deadline, is usually better than a July event. Additionally, I'm sure that Kingsford Charcoal doesn't sponsor too many skiing promotions!

4. Does the property have national appeal to consumers and therefore broader promotional implications? . Just as NASCAR may be ideal from a loyalty perspective, it may be less than ideal if the sponsor is running a sweepstakes promotion and needs to appeal to consumers in the Pacific Northwest (not a NASCAR hotbed) just as much as in the Southeast (NASCAR's roots).

5. If the event/property is national, does it have regional or local extension opportunities? An NFL relationship allows sponsors to not only reach the "national"

NFL fan/consumer, but also 30 different local consumer markets (Bears, Cowboys, etc.), with attendant local programs. Conversely, at present, a Major League Soccer relationship delivers a sponsor a limited number of markets, not all of them "A" markets.

6. Does the sponsorship allow the sponsor to re-coup its investment through sales of product or self-liquidating offers? Sponsorships are increasingly more expensive. Can the sponsor sell product at the event? Can the sponsor "sell" third party pass-through rights to retailers or vendors so as to mitigate costs (similar to what Home Depot did with its $40 million Olympic commitment, selling Olympic promotional rights to Home Depot vendors)?

7. Does the property appeal to employees, especially salespeople, so that it can be used as motivation and/or an incentive to satisfy internal business objectives? Many companies are sponsors of a property solely so they can use attendance at a Championship game as an incentive tool for their sales force.

8. Does the property create trade/entertainment hospitality vehicles? Are there exclusive, perceived high-value entertainment opportunities with the sponsorship (suites, VIP passes, unique experiences)? How many tickets are included and do they have a high perceived value to the trade so that they can be leveraged for incremental support?

9. Does the property provide for account-specific promotion opportunities? Today, most retailers want a unique promotion with which to speak to their respective customer base (Target and Wal-Mart certainly want to distinguish themselves from one another). Therefore, vendors that supply promotions to these retailers need to give each retailer as unique a promotion as possible. Those properties that provide a variety of different "legs" that can then be passed along to different retailers are of the greatest benefit.

10. Does the property block out the competition? Can the sponsor have category exclusively? Are the categories defined narrowly or broadly (automotive vs. imported car/domestic car/truck, imaging vs. cameras/film/videotape)?

11. What are the costs associated with leveraging the sponsorship? Is there an appropriate cost/benefit relationship for participating and leveraging? How expensive is the base sponsorship? How encompassing (signage at the events, logo usage, etc.)? How much more has to be spent to leverage the property?

12. What is the clutter factor? Is the property selective about number and type of sponsors/ messages? How many other sponsors are there? If many, is there an opportunity to create or own a proprietary element within the property so as to stand out more (e.g., Texaco not only sponsors MLB, but "owns" All-Star balloting; True Value is not only a sponsor of the NFL, but "owns" the Man of the Year Charity Award).

13. Does having a relationship with the event or property help generate positive non-paid media/PR? Does the property receive extensive exposure for itself and/or the charitable programs associated with it? If so, how can the sponsor leverage this into additional awareness and positive publicity?

14. Does the property market and promote aggressively? To what extent is the property being promoted to its fullest potential? How is it perceived overall? Are the property owners/executives strategic marketers who can help build the property and the sponsor along with it (NBA)? Will the sponsor have to spend too much time worrying about how well the event manager is marketing the event?

15. Does the property facilitate a positive cooperative working relationship? How hard is it to get things done with the property personnel? Are they easy to work with? Many people in our business would be surprised if they knew how often sponsors select one property over another based on the ease/difficulty of working with the property personnel.

By understanding these criteria, combined with your knowledge of the sponsor's business, you can develop a sponsorship offering that meets the sponsor's needs.

Chapter 25 – SELLING SPONSORSHIPS MADE EASY

With the continuing dramatic growth of sponsorship of everything from local little league baseball teams to the Olympics, a lot of people are attempting to sell sponsorship to companies. The standard way is to write a lengthy proposal listing all the sponsorship levels available, mail it out with a cover letter to a name from a master mailing list, and <u>maybe</u> follow up with a phone call. Effective? Hardly!

Sponsorship sales is like any other selling process. You must understand your product (the event, sport, arts or entertainment project you are trying to sell); you must understand how your product meets their marketing needs. Sounds simple, doesn't it? However, most sponsorship salespeople only go through the first step, understanding the product they are selling.

In order to be effective at sponsorship sales, you must first be a salesperson. Take some sales training, understand what it is to be a consultative salesperson, discover the art of overcoming objections, and learn how to tailor your sponsorship to meet the sponsor's needs while, at the same time, meeting the needs of your event. This applies to events, sports, arts, CRM and entertainment.

When determining who you are going to approach for sponsorship, DO YOUR HOMEWORK. Get a copy of the annual report, request copies of their marketing materials, do a data search at the library, discover what their marketing strategies and approaches are for the coming year. Does your event fit those strategies? Can it be tailored to match those strategies? Or, is it in total opposition to what they want to achieve? If that is the case, don't waste any more time on that sponsor. Go on and find out who is qualified to become a sponsor for your event.

Once you have the necessary background to discuss the company intelligently, call your appropriate contact within the company and discuss your project with him/her. Ask if you can meet to discuss your project. If the contact requests information, fax or e-mail a brief, one-page fact sheet (Appendix B). Then, follow up for further discussion. Don't waste your time, energy or money on a voluminous proposal that resembles the first draft of *War and Peace* if the sponsor isn't interested!

Let's take it from the point where the sponsor *is* interested. Be prepared with a full proposal that relates the specific sponsor needs and benefits as they pertain to your event when you go into your presentation meeting. This should contain relevant materials from the annual report, marketing materials, and data gathered from your initial telephone conversations. Be prepared to negotiate a package that is mutually beneficial. Take time to listen to the potential sponsor's needs and attempt to incorporate those requests into your sponsorship proposal.

Okay ... you're successful and you have your sponsors. Your work has just begun. During the entire process from pre-event to post-event you will be in close contact with your sponsors. You will involve them in the production process, maintain contact through creative material execution to ensure adherence to their graphic standards, include them in all public relations activities, and make sure every element in their sponsorship package is delivered. And, when everything is over, you will provide each sponsor with a post-event summary and report.

This, of course, is a very brief overview of sponsorship sales. However, it addresses some of the major pitfalls and problems currently encountered by people attempting to sell sponsorships. This is a very targeted, sponsor-specific approach that gives a much greater return on time and energy than some of the current methods. This whole process is greatly enhanced if undertaken by someone who is a sales professional.

Selling sponsorships is great fun and certainly rewarding, both financially and emotionally. Selling <u>properly</u> just enhances these benefits.

Chapter 26 – WHAT SPONSOR'S *DON'T* WANT TO HEAR

One of the major problems sponsorship salespeople have is taking time to listen to the potential sponsor and determine what's important to them. Rather, they present their credentials, list a number of benefits for a range of sponsorship options in a sponsorship "package", and hope that the person will buy. As you know by now, rigid, delineated, outlined sponsorship "packages" are almost passé. Rather, consultative sponsorship salespeople are taking time to find out what sponsors want and tailoring a program to meet those particular needs.

Following are some of the sponsorship benefits that are listed in "packages" that have little or no value to a sponsor. These are actual examples from recent sponsorship packages received by potential sponsors. And, in the parentheses you will find their comments:

- Your logo on all banners. (OK, now what? What is the exposure, what is the competition, where are the banners being placed, etc.?)

- Your logo on all press releases. (Does that guarantee that the media will acknowledge that sponsorship? Probably not.)

- Your logo on all promotional material. (What material? Who does it go to? What is the value to me [as sponsor]?)

- Right to place banner at your booth. (I would hope so! They are paying for the space!)

- Event will endeavor to publicize major sponsors' involvement with the event. (Again, what does this mean? Be specific in your definition ... this is too fuzzy to mean anything.)

- Positive public awareness. (What does this mean?)

- Great exposure. (How? Measured? What media?)

- Millions of impressions (For the sponsor or the event! Be specific.)

When developing your sponsorship options, think like your potential sponsors. Understand their business, their marketing objectives, their target markets and be prepared to address their specific needs with your benefits. It can be easy!

Chapter 27 – WHY SPONSORS RENEW/BUY

Following are marketers' top reasons for renewing event sponsorships:

1. Property fulfills contractual obligations;
2. Sponsorship fee is reasonable;
3. Amount of media coverage - event;
4. Amount of media coverage - sponsor;
5. Treatment by promoter;
6. Amount of signage;
7. Total attendance;
8. Audience's demographic/psychographic composition;
9. Type of media;
10. Increased sales;
11. Types of other sponsors;
12. Cross-promotion with other sponsors;
13. Feedback from guests/employees;
14. Entertain guests;
15. Access to rail, so material can be easily shipped;
16. On-site sampling;
17. Experiential marketing opportunity.

Notice how important the fulfillment of contractual obligations is to the sponsor!

Now, here are some of the most common reasons marketers sponsor events:

1. Increase sales;
2. Increase awareness of company or product name;
3. Identification with a particular lifestyle;
4. Differentiate product from competitors;
5. Enhance commitment to community or ethnic group;
6. Entertain key clients; business-to-business marketing;
7. Merchandising opportunities;
8. Shape or reinforce the public's perception of a product's attributes;

9. Impact the bottom line.

If you keep these ideas in mind when calling on sponsors, it will help you be more effective at partnering with them.

Chapter 28 – SPONSORS WANT A RETURN ON (THEIR) INVESTMENT (ROI)

When selling a sponsorship, take time at the beginning of the relationship to determine what measurements are important to the sponsor. This conversation should involve the definition of objectives, the establishment of a pre-sponsorship benchmark against which to measure, and the maintenance of consistent levels of advertising and promotion to isolate the impact of the sponsorship. Three of the most common sponsorship objectives are to change or reinforce the image of their brand, influence the trade and increase sales. But, how do you measure these objectives?

Imposing the familiar advertising models onto sponsorship is not the answer. Just as TV wasn't merely radio with pictures, sponsorship is not just advertising with added value.

The real issue for today's sponsors is ROI. To justify expenditures, sponsors must show that associating with this NFL team or that street festival positions their products or services so that consumers want to buy them, while influencing the key elements in the sales chain so that there is a readily available outlet from which to buy.

Sponsorship return can be measured. The key lies in defining objectives, establishing a pre-sponsorship benchmark against which to measure, and maintaining consistent levels of advertising and promotion so that it is possible to isolate the effect of the sponsorship.

The lack of a universal system for measuring sponsorship is a problem, but it is also an opportunity. Often a sponsorship is dropped - not because there is no measurable value - because no one has taken time to measure the value! [Ed. Note: That's why the post-event report is so important!] This lack of a single, standardized measurement is also an opportunity because it means sponsors and events can tailor the measurement systems to specific objectives.

Here is a suggested way to measure the three most common sponsorship objectives:

1. Measuring attitudinal change. Companies often use sponsorship to position or change the image attributes of their company brand. This type of measurement calls for pre- and post-attitude studies. Before launching a tie-in, the sponsor must determine attitudes and image perceptions among their targets and set goal levels the sponsorship is expected to achieve. Another survey is conducted after the sponsorship to determine if the goals were met.

2. Measuring impact on the trade. Companies using sponsorship to influence their distribution channel can compare the number of retailers or dealers participating in their sponsorship-themed program to the number which typically participate in a standard program; track the number of new outlets carrying their product; or measure incremental displays at the point-of-purchase. Again, it is vital to measure both pre- and post-event for an accurate measurement.

3. Measuring sales increases to end-users. Sponsorship can be tied directly to sales so that companies can measure not only how many people were reached but, as well, how many were actually motivated to buy. Methods for measuring this objective include comparing sales for the two-to-three month period surrounding the sponsorship to the same period in previous years; measuring sales in the immediate event area against national sales; and tying sales directly to the sponsored event (for example, ticket discount with proof of purchase), then tracking redemptions.

A variation of this involves working with your sales force to trace the value of leads and contacts generated by a sponsorship.

What do you learn from this?

- Does event sponsorship pay off? You don't know until you measure, and measuring can be tricky!

- If you measure merely in terms of CPM you won't get a clear analysis unless, of course, your only reason for sponsoring is to generate gross impressions.

- There's no universal benchmark for measuring sponsorships. That's a problem but also an opportunity since it allows you to tailor a measurement system to address specific sponsor objectives.

Summary

Working with your sponsor, develop measurable goals and objectives before the event. Then, design a measurement that will accurately reflect the impact of the sponsorship on those goals and objectives. Keep in mind that the three key measurement values are impact on the consumer, impact on the trade, and impact on sales.

Chapter 29 – INTEGRATION: THE KEY TO SUCCESSFUL SPONSORSHIP (from the sponsor's point-of-view)

One of today's hottest buzzwords in advertising is integration. How does it work with sponsorship? Exactly the same way it does with all elements of your marketing program.

Integrated marketing is simply making sure that you have a consistency of message, design and program so that your message is easily identified and recognized by your target customers. This means that your print ads will have a theme that is consistent with your electronic media advertising and all the elements -- posters, flyers, bill stuffers, you name it -- will be uniform in their marketing message and benefits orientation. In addition, your sales promotion strategy will dovetail with the various marketing elements to provide a single "face" to your customers.

To be effective in sponsorship, you must make the same attempts to be uniform and consistent in your marketing efforts and interweave your event/sport sponsorship program into a virtually seamless program. For example, if you have determined that an arts sponsorship will help you reach your target customers, you will want to integrate all the elements of that sponsorship into your existing advertising program. If you have entered into the agreement soon enough, the integration process is more easily accomplished than jumping into an event at the last minute and trying to make everything work together.

Why have you undertaken this particular sponsorship? Does it reach your customers? Are you introducing a new brand to a new target market? Does the event fit neatly into your existing marketing strategy? What steps are necessary to implement your sponsorship in a way consistent with your current marketing program? What results do you want?

Today's sponsorships must offer results. Gone are the days of the CEO's decision to sponsor golf because he loves to play golf! (Or, **almost** gone!) Businesses today want accountability and measurement: did the sponsorship increase sales? improve profitability? enhance image? etc. Accountability and measurement are enhanced when the sponsorship is a comfortable (and logical) fit with the total marketing strategy.

Here are some key questions to ask a company when considering a sponsorship proposal. If the answer to any of these is "no," they will probably have more difficulty integrating your sponsorship into their total marketing plan than if the answer is "yes."

1. Does the lifestyle event reach our defined target market?

2. Does it offer us a media package that enhances our current marketing efforts?

3. Are the on-site opportunities compatible with our current program?

4. Does the event/sport provide us with a value-added program that will effectively extend our marketing program?

5. Can we measure the results of our participation?

6. Will the event organizers work with us on planning and implementation of marketing strategies that are consistent with our marketing philosophy?

7. Can we extend the value of our sponsorship with pre- and post-event programs?

8. Does the hospitality package have true value in impacting our bottom line?

9. Is the event looking for a long-term relationship?

Of course, you can think of more but these basic questions will help you quickly understand when a company decides whether or not to continue negotiations for a particular sponsorship.

These rules apply for the sponsoring organization as well. The National Basketball Association is an excellent example of an organization that has applied the principles and practices of integrated marketing and been very successful at it. All marketing activities are designed with the total marketing picture in mind and cross all lines, from design and production of tickets, through licensed products and sales, to video production.

A leading sponsor recently stated, "Integration is paramount. Sponsorships must conform to a brand's overall positioning and objectives to be worth the increasingly higher price tags they command."

If you are involved in sponsorship sales, understanding the marketing strategies of your target companies will help you be more effective in designing a sponsorship proposal that will be perceived as having marketing value. For example, if you are going to approach VISA International for a sponsorship, study their annual report, research their current marketing programs, review their marketing materials, and attempt to reach the decision-maker **before** sending out the materials. You might discover that there are elements in your program that are not consistent with the marketing objectives of that company, which would then either allow you to modify your sponsorship so it can be integrated into their program or contact someone else for whom the sponsorship would be more compatible.

With the continued growth of sponsorship opportunities, and companies demanding greater and greater accountability and results, integration of sponsorships into the total marketing program will continue to grow in importance. Taking time to determine how your program can be integrated into a sponsor's existing marketing strategy will enhance your ability to make that sponsorship work - for you and for the sponsor.

Chapter 30 – REMEMBER - THE SPONSOR WALKS ON WATER

Yes, without your event, there would be nothing to sponsor. However, without the sponsor's dollars, you wouldn't have an event. In this chicken/egg scenario, let's take the sponsor's side and talk about the importance of sponsorship and the client servicing aspects of sponsorship.

When negotiating with your sponsors, always keep them informed of what is happening. The more they are involved in the process, the more interested they become in your project. And, the greater the involvement, the greater the commitment.

Once your sponsor has agreed to some level of participation, make sure both parties understand who is doing what and for how much. Put it in writing and outline it in great detail - there is nothing worse than making an assumption that something will be taken care of and find out, too late, that it has been neglected. And, once it is in writing, have both sides sign and acknowledge that, indeed, this is what has been agreed upon and is to be adhered to.

When incorporating a corporate sponsor's logo into your promotional material, make sure you have a copy of their graphics standards manual so you know what can and cannot be done with the logo. A nice touch is to have the sponsors look at your creative before it goes to print and just sign off on how their logo is positioned. With the ability to fax or e-mail at a moment's notice, this sign-off/approval process can be done quickly and easily.

Include the sponsor in your planning meetings, add them to your memo distribution list, and make sure they receive all press mailings, advisories and notices. When you start receiving media reports of coverage, make copies for the sponsors and mail to them.

During the event, assign someone to be directly responsive to the sponsor's wishes and needs. Make sure this is a willing, energetic and tactful representative who has been totally apprised of their particular sponsor's benefits and is qualified to solve any problems that might arise.

What problems? Something as simple as the assigned priority parking spot has been taken by someone else; the food for the hospitality tent has not arrived on time; the correct number of tickets to the event have not been given to the sponsor; one of the banners is missing; on-site signage has been placed incorrectly; the sponsor's name is mispronounced on the audio billboard, etc, Those of you who have been involved in sponsorship can certainly add your own items to this list.

And, what about the rights the sponsor **thinks** should be his/hers? Be prepared to deal with the unexpected by having a senior event person available as an onsite resource to the sponsor. Make sure problems are solved quickly, quietly and amicably. For example, the sponsor benefit they are asking for may not be part of the contract; however the sponsor is your customer and the customer is always right. Take efforts to resolve the debatable point in a way that is mutually agreeable. If you have to, err on the side of the sponsor. The payback will be terrific, as the sponsors will remember the event in a positive manner, which will certainly contribute to their desire to renew.

Make sure you take plenty of pictures of the event. This includes crowd shots, pictures of celebrities, and various activities. Always take pictures of each sponsor as you will need those photos for your post-event report. In addition, collect sufficient collateral - ticket stubs, program books, flyers, etc. – to include in the post-event report.

Then, when the event is over, provide your sponsor(s) with a full report on the event, making sure you include all those elements previously agreed upon. After each one, recap how those benefits were met (and, in many cases, exceeded) by the event and its management. Provide the sponsor with a written and visual diary of the event with attendance figures, event highlights and actual exposure all tied together into an event summary that documents the sponsor's involvement and benefits.

Selling the sponsorship is merely the first step. Implementation, the execution of the many details of the sponsorship program, is the most important step. In fact, poor implementation will result in an unhappy sponsor who will probably not return to the next event. Conversely, if all involved pay attention to the details and implementation runs smoothly, the sponsor will probably continue his/her affiliation with your event.

Chapter 31 – HOW TO MAKE EFFECTIVE SPONSOR-SHIP PRESENTATIONS

Sooner or later, when soliciting sponsorship, you will be asked to make a formal appearance before a group to present your concepts and ideas. To be effective, do your homework before you go into that meeting. It will be the difference between a "Don't call us, we'll call you" response and a resounding "Yes!"

1. Know Your Property

Sponsors want to know all the components of your event. How many people will be attending? What is the past history of the event? Who were the previous sponsors? What media relationships have been established? Will there be TV coverage and are spots being made available to sponsors? What are the demographics of attendees and participants?

Potential sponsors are particularly interested in the results of market research. If you have had Chilton, Joyce Julius, or any of the other market research companies that specialize in market research do research on your event, be sure to mention that fact and share the results with your sponsors. Be prepared to offer marketing and promotion ideas that will enhance their sponsorship and provide them with a good, measurable return on their investment.

2. Know Your Potential Sponsor

We can't say it enough times ... know your sponsors. Read their annual reports, study the trade publications to see what their marketing efforts have been over the last year, learn about their distribution channels, become familiar with their product lines (new and old) ... in short, understand their business as well as they do.

Talk to the people involved in sponsorship. Discuss their marketing needs and your event. Working with them, try to determine how their participation in your event can be win/win for both sides. This dialogue is vital for the success of your presentation and their participation. It is this pre-sell period that gets them interested in your event and motivates them to have you make a full presentation to their peers and corporate decision-makers.

Then, match their business to your event. What elements are you offering that will help them meet their marketing objectives? What components of your sponsorship will help them increase a current brand's awareness, introduce a new product or introduce a line extension of a current product?

3. Know How to be an Effective Presenter

Prepare your material; rehearse your material. When making your presentation, be sure to establish eye contact with each and every person in the room. Don't focus on just one person. You don't know who the key decision-maker will be and focusing on one person not only makes that person uncomfortable but everyone else in the room.

Talk slowly. At whatever pace you are speaking, slow it down. Pause between paragraphs ... give your information time to sink in. **STAND STILL!** Many people shift from foot to foot in a weaving, bobbing manner. If you have to, envision that both feet are mailed to the floor and you cannot move! Any kind of physical distraction detracts from your words and your concept.

Eliminate "ummmmm" and "and uh....". As stated earlier, rehearse your material. Tape-record your rehearsal. Listen to yourself. Become acutely aware of word patterns. Rehearse and tape until you have almost eliminated them.

4. Know When to Stop

Remember the KISS theory? Keep It Short and Simple. You should be able to present any sponsorship concept, in a formal presentation, in 30 minutes. Don't belabor all the points; don't dwell on minutiae; don't bore your audience with meaningless statistics. Leave them wanting more information and interested enough to ask questions.

5. Be Prepared to Answer Questions

If you have presented your material in an interesting, cohesive and appropriate manner, there will be questions. If, by some chance you get a question for which you don't have the answer, say so. Tell them you will find out and get back to them within 24 hours. Then, go on to the next questions. Don't dwell on the fact you don't have the answer and don't try to make up an answer. Your honesty will be appreciated.

6. Suggested Format to Follow

Start with a brief overview of the event ... history, past event highlights, attendance, media coverage, and previous sponsors (5 minutes). Next, present a synopsis of your findings about the sponsorship company ... marketing goals, target markets, products, etc. (5 minutes). Follow this with a presentation of your sponsorship suggestion and the component parts (10 minutes). Give a brief overview of your organization - history, experience, successes, relationship to event, etc. (5 minutes). Then, go into your conclusion, summarizing the various elements and tying them together into a closing statement where you ask for the sale (5 minutes).

Summary

Making an effective sponsorship presentation, then, consists of a number of components including knowing the property you are selling, understanding your potential sponsors' wants and needs, being an effective presenter, handling questions in a professional and educated manner, and presenting the material in a logical format that keeps the listeners interested. The sure sign of an effective sponsorship presentation? When they say "yes"!

Chapter 32 – HOW TO WRITE A SPONSORSHIP LETTER THAT GETS RESPONSE...COVER LETTERS THAT WORK!

The cover letter you send with your sponsorship proposal can often make the difference between getting your sponsorship offering read and receiving a nice "thanks but no thanks" letter. What makes the difference between a "good" sponsorship letter and a "bad" one? The same things that make the difference between a "good" sales letter and a "bad" one.

When preparing your event's sponsorship offering, you took great care to outline the various sponsorship elements and the benefits they provide. You carefully packaged the media, hospitality, sales promotion, signage and on-site offerings to provide a fair and equitable opportunity, whether title sponsorship or one of the supporting sponsorship deals. You researched your potential market to identify which sponsors would be most qualified to participate; which ones had audience and marketing needs that were parallel to those of your sponsorship offering. In short, you did your homework.

Then, you quickly wrote a generic cover letter that allowed you to customize each package by name and company and mailed them off. This mailing was then followed by a series of telephone calls to the people who received the sponsorship offerings to determine their interest. If you did not have a good cover letter, and had not prequalified the potential sponsors before the mailing, you probably experienced a low interest/response to your mailing. Next time, apply the following principles of good sales letter writing and you'll see a difference in the response!

Rule #1

Make sure you have the proper spelling of the person's name, title, and company as well as a correct address. If you have to call and confirm this information before mailing, do so.

Rule #2

Eliminate as many references to "I", "me" or "my" as possible. Here's an example of a terrible paragraph:

"I would like to have an opportunity to sit down and show you why my event is so important. I've worked on this for over 5 years and I need to have at least 10 sponsors who will give me $100,000 so I can have a successful event."

Six times in one paragraph ... not good!

Rule #3

Make sure your letter is benefits oriented. And, the benefits orientation must be custom tailored. Don't make the following mistake:

"Title Sponsorship of $100,000 for XYZ Event offers your organization exclusive rights to distribute the product of your choice."

Instead, take time to know your potential sponsor. The above paragraph would be written differently for each sponsor with specific elements itemized. For example, assume that XYZ Event is looking for a carbonated beverage sponsor. And, further, let's assume the targeted carbonated beverage sponsors are Coca-Cola, RC Cola and Cadbury Schweppes Ginger Ale. Each of these companies has a different marketing strategy and need. The above paragraph would be written as follows for each of these potential sponsors:

Coca-Cola

"As title sponsor of the XYZ Event, Coca-Cola would continue their dominance of the XYZ market as well as enjoying exclusive pouring rights at the XYZ Event. With event attendance estimated at _____ (number of attendees) and the audience primarily consisting of young men and women ages 18-35, you have an ideal opportunity to get exposure for _____(specific name of product)."

RC Cola

"As title sponsor of XYZ Event, RC Cola would be presented with the opportunity to have exclusive beverage rights at an event that attracts your competition's primary market. Between in-store promotions, product sales, signage and sampling opportunities, XYZ Event offers RC Cola an opportunity to dramatically impact sales."

Cadbury Schweppes Ginger Ale

"XYZ Event offers Cadbury Schweppes Ginger Ale an opportunity to market to their target audience ... young men and women ages 18-35 ... plus have the bonus opportunity of trade promotions. Title sponsorship would give Cadbury Schweppes exclusive pouring rights for Ginger Ale as well as signage, trade hospitality, and new-product sampling."

As you can see, specific benefits as they relate to the specific company are provided in the cover letter.

Rule #4

Never make a statement that is general in nature and that cannot be substantiated by solid facts. For example:

"The response to the event has been terrific and the support by other sponsors is overwhelming. All the media are excited about participating in XYZ Event."

This is fluff. Rather, this same paragraph could be written as follows:

"The initial mailing to 100 sponsors has provided us with at least 20 major companies who are interested in some level of participation in XYZ Event. These sponsors include such well-known names as _____, _____ and _____. In addition, _____newspaper, _____radio station and _____ TV will be providing extensive coverage of XYZ Event. All of this has a

72

positive impact by generating more interest in a greater attendance at XYZ Event. Through your sponsorship of this event, you too will benefit from this exposure and attendance."

Rule #5

Always state when you will follow up with them; never make it their responsibility to call you. For example:

"Thanks for your interest and I look forward to hearing from you."

Rather, word the final paragraph this way:

"Thanks for taking time to read this proposal and seeing how XYZ Event offers (name of company) a viable lifestyle marketing opportunity. I will call you the week of (date) to discuss the feasibility of our meeting to discuss this further."

You should put as much effort into your cover letter as you do the whole proposal. Research your sponsors: find out what their marketing strategies are and what products are logical choices for your event sponsorship. Understand their marketing needs and tailor your letter to satisfy their needs. Eliminate I/me/my from your focus ... begin to think in terms of "you" and have a strong benefits orientation. And, don't think this letter can be written quickly. It might take 3 or 4 hours to craft a good letter that will create interest in your event, inspire the reader to go through the proposal, and generate a desire to discuss it further. That time will be well invested if you are successful in generating sponsorship dollars for your event.

The major don't? Don't make up form letter, buy a mailing list, use mail merge and send out the letter with the name dropped into the various blanks…you won't get any response and it's a waste of time and money!

Here are a dozen powerful (and effective) phrases. Use as needed and where valid!

1. Measurable response
2. Qualified media coverage
3. Diverse, integrated marketing opportunities
4. Improve market share
5. Targeted marketing messages
6. Database marketing opportunities
7. Generous hospitality components
8. Increase product exposure
9. Enhance existing marketing efforts
10. Develop qualified sales leads
11. Solidify client relationships
12. Increase sales!

Chapter 33 – FIVE MINUTES IS ALL YOU'VE GOT!

Or, how to make sure your prospect understands your sponsorship.

Events need sponsors to survive, and more and more people are vying for available sponsorship dollars -- no news here. And you've all seen the sponsorship proposals prospective sponsors receive offering them "Title," "Presenting Sponsor," "Associate Sponsor," and so on. Or, maybe different dollar levels are represented by such exciting categories as "Platinum," "Gold," etc. Often these proposals are many pages long, with much of the information hidden within the text. They all suffer from the following:

1. They are all too wordy;

2. Event details are difficult to extract from the total presentation;

3. Glitzy presentations take the place of factual information;

4. The information is obscure at best!

When your prospective sponsors receive your information, you've probably got only five minutes of their time to make an impression. How can you get your message across in that time period? By presenting your material in an easy-to-read, benefits-oriented, orderly manner. And one of the easiest ways to do this is to provide, at the beginning of your proposal, either an Executive Summary or a simple Event Fact Sheet. Either of these should be no more than one page and offer, in itemized fashion, the highlights of your proposal.

What should be included? The recommended basic areas are: target audience, location, date/time/year, marketing and merchandising opportunities, hospitality, and media.

Target Audience

Who will be attending? What age groups are involved? Break down total exposure by attendees, participants, sponsors, media and event management. With some sponsors, quantity of exposures is important; with others, quality is more important. By defining your total target audience, you make it easier for the sponsor to make an initial decision on participation.

Location

Simply, where will the event be held? And, remember that the person may not be familiar with the location, so provide the name and address, including city and state. You are very familiar with your own property -- don't assume the recipient of your sponsorship offering is too!

Date/Time/Year

Simplistic? Maybe. Except that many of the proposals hide that information on page 10! Remember, the easier it is for the person to read, the easier it is for him/her to say "Yes."

Marketing and Merchandising Opportunities

Let your potential sponsors know the various opportunities that are available. Can they have signage? If yes, what size, how many, and where? Or, can they do product sampling, product sales, couponing, displays, audio announcements, etc.? Since this is a single-page fact sheet summarizing the vital statistics of your sponsorship offering, just list the items as bullets. Use your proposal to provide detailed explanations of the various opportunities.

Hospitality

Can your sponsors have tickets to the event/game? What about hospitality tents/suites, or a special opportunity to meet the stars (breakfast with... etc.)? Again, just bullet items and explain within the proposal.

Media

What media are involved? Is there a print/electronic/out-of-home media package that will enhance their sponsorship commitment? Be brief in this fact sheet because the objective is to provide an overview that will entice them to continue reading.

Keep in mind that many of the people involved in the sponsorship decision receive as many as 10,000 proposals a year. Assuming they work 200 days a year (with time out for sick days, vacation, travel, seminars and events) that would mean they evaluate 40 proposals a day. In an 8 hour day, they are able to devote 10 minutes to each one! I don't think so! By making your proposal clear, concise and easy to read, you multiply your chances for further exploration and success. Obscure the facts, and expect your proposal to go nowhere but the round file.

Chapter 34 – BASIC PROMOTION IDEAS

Sponsorship is no longer a matter of hanging your banner, getting a bunch of seats on the 50-yard line, and meeting the star players. Sports and special events are now part of the marketing mix and are expected to **deliver**. For that reason, you will be asked to incorporate various types of promotions as part of your total sponsorship package. Here are some basic ideas that can be used singly or combined in any number of ways that will help you achieve marketing success. Once you have pursued all the combinations you will have hundreds of cross-promotion ideas that work!

1. Bouncebacks - Using something at the event to bring the customer back to the store. For example, bring your ticket stub to XYZ store and redeem for **your** product. Or, at some time during the event, give the customer a coupon that is a special offering and is redeemable after the event. It literally "bounces the customer back" to the retail store and allows the product sponsor to measure the sales effectiveness of his/her sponsorship as well as the retail store's ability to do the same.

2. Buy One, Get One Free (BOGO) - Taken alone, this is a product sale enticement. If combined with one of the other elements of sales promotion, it can not only increase product sales but also tie in with your event sponsorship. For example, as part of the BOGO promotion, you receive a sweepstakes entry form for a free trip, free tickets, etc., (whatever you wish).

3. Contests/Sweepstakes - These can be unlimited! You can have registration at the point-of-purchase, at the event, even through the mail. One word of caution - don't undertake a contest without consulting a lawyer since each state has very specific rules about entry requirements, probability of winning clauses, etc.

4. Coupons - These can be either pre-event or at the event. If they are distributed through a retail facility, they can be used to promote your sponsorship before an event and, hopefully, to drive additional traffic to the event. In fact, the coupon could be distributed through your retail partner and used for event admission discounts. Or, coupons can be distributed at the event to drive sales after the event.

5. Database Development - As more and more companies get involved in marketing directly to their customers, take advantage of generating a list of your customers' names. Have a booth at your event where people can participate in a survey, enter a contest, or just register to win with hourly drawings at the event.

6. Discounted Sales - Taken alone, they're a way to drive traffic into a store. Combined with a coupon or bounceback, they are a way to reward an event attendee with an additional "bonus" for attending that event. Then, combine it with a "register to win" promotion and you not only measure the results of attendance at your sponsored event but also generate names for your database.

7. FSIs (Free Standing Inserts) - These can combine coupons, register to win, sweepstakes, contests, etc. They are the four-color advertising-only inserts that are so prevalent in your Sunday paper. For Super Bowl alone this year a number of

Super Bowl sponsors participated in a 36-page FSI that was distributed nationally one week before the big game.

8. Hang Tags - Literally, tags that hang off the product. These can be used with soft goods and food products, particularly bottled beverages. Again, design the tag like a coupon to drive traffic to the event, or an entry form to win tickets to the event, whatever you want.

9. Internet - The entire cyberspace concept is wide open for sales promotion ideas. Special offers or discounts, pre-event, can be designed as well as additional sponsor/event information that would entice customers to the event as well as encourage them to purchase the product. Add to this advertising banners, hyperlinks to sponsor sights and the other range of options and you have a powerful promotion tool.

10. Media Coupons - Similar to FSIs, these are coupons that are included in coupon mailings, newspaper and magazine ads, and other print coupon distribution. Again, use them like coupons or bouncebacks to enhance pre- and post-event sales and participation.

11. On-Air Promotions - Using radio, television and cable, you can make the same offers as you would with coupons only using the electronic media. Same activity and results as in #10.

12. On-Pack Promotions - These are special offers on the product package. They can either be cut out or easily peeled off and are similar to coupons and bouncebacks to generate pre- and post-event coverage as well as database development.

13. On-Site Sampling - Use your sponsorship to either sample a new product or introduce consumers to a new product application through sampling. This can be actually tasting a product or giving a demonstration. Combine this with bouncebacks and/or a register-to-win promotion and you have additional sales as well as development of a potential customer database.

14. Phone Cards - Pre-paid phone cards can be distributed at the event -- with the sponsor's name clearly in evidence -- and used to drive customers back to the sponsor's place of business in order to get their pin code activated. Or, they can be distributed before the event with the requirement that the consumer attend the event to get their specific pin code activated.

15. Point-of-Purchase Tie-Ins - These can consist of instant coupons at the checkout counter, on-shelf promotions, end cap displays with "take ones," etc. Again, combine with some of the other sales promotion ideas to enhance results.

16. Point-of-Purchase Promotions - These can include product sampling with coupons, point-of-sale promotions, contests, etc. And, point-of-purchase can be at your retail partner's location before the event or at the event itself.

17. Product Promotions - These can include on-pack coupons or entry forms, register receipt with UPC codes, or any other form of promotion that is specifically tied to

proof of purchase. As with contests, check with your lawyer on the exact wording and application to ensure that you are not violating the law.

18. Product Sales - Very simply, sell your product at the event! This is a viable sponsorship benefit and allows you to add one of the other promotion ideas presented here - coupons, bouncebacks, register to win, contests - to measure impact and effectiveness.

19. Shelf Talkers/Take-Ones - These are point-of-purchase promotions, usually right where the product is located on the retail shelves, with additional incentive for purchase. Similar to coupons and bouncebacks with similar applications.

You have the basics, now let your imagination run wild! Any number of combinations will help you successfully drive product sales, measure effectiveness of your sponsorship investment, and even increase event attendance. Good luck!

Chapter 35 – HOW _NOT_ TO SELL YOUR SPONSORSHIPS

If you are an event organizer involved in sponsorship sales, you have probably experienced the challenge of sponsorship solicitation. If you have practiced the norm, you have probably designed a sponsorship package with a range of options available (title, presenting sponsorship, associate, etc.); written a basic, generic cover letter; looked up the appropriate names in the various directories listing sponsorship contacts (_IEG, Team Marketing Report, Entertainment Marketing Sourcebook, etc._); put together media clippings and other appropriate support documentation; packaged the whole thing and mailed it off to several hundred selected sponsors.

After an appropriate time, you may or may not have followed up with a telephone call asking, "Did you get the package? What do you think?" In many instances, you discovered they had not received the package or, more appropriately, did not remember receiving the package. Your sales call is now blocked until they have the proposal in front of them and can relate to it. So, you send them another one and the cycle begins again. Bottom line? Time and money invested for a limited return and you have allowed the sponsor to take charge of the sales call.

Is this a good way to sell sponsorships? Not really. In today's fast-paced, high-tech, massive-information world, there is a better, more effective way to sell sponsorships. It requires more work at the front end, before you send out your sponsorship proposals, but your sponsorship sales success ratio will be much higher.

The first step in sponsorship sales is to analyze your event from the sponsor's perspective. As we discussed previously, look at your event through a sponsor's eyes. Who is attending? What is your audience profile? Your participant's profile? Is your event attracting 25-34 year old males, 55+ active seniors, children 6-12, or another combination that reflects your event?

Once you have profiled your event, research those companies that you think might be interested in sponsorship, either because you have seen them participate in something similar or you know that they have products/services that appeal to your particular event's audience.

When the research is completed, and you have determined not only the companies you want to participate as sponsors but also who the contact people are, call them up. Talk to them before mailing out any material to them. Do a preliminary qualification call to determine 1) if they are interested and, assuming yes, 2) in what way they are interested. The initial qualification process is a matter of asking questions that relate to the research you have done and consists of a series of questions that will help you formulate a better picture of what sponsorship opportunities are best suited to this company. **Listen to the answers**. As Tom Hopkins, a famous (and successful) salesperson says, "We have two ears and one mouth which means we should listen twice as much as we speak!"

Once you have done the preliminary qualification, you are ready to take the next step. Assuming interest on the part of the potential sponsoring organization, ask them if they would like additional information. If yes, send them a one-page fact sheet via fax or e-mail, and immediately follow up with a telephone call. Make sure they understand the event and the opportunities that are presented before continuing to the next step.

Your next step is to make every effort to get an appointment for a personal visit (assuming it is geographically and/or economically feasible. If the sponsorship stakes are high enough, flying to the potential sponsor's location is not out of the question). Once the appointment is made, you have two options: the first is to tailor your sponsorship offering to that specific sponsor's needs, as expressed to you during the qualification process, and send it to him/her prior to your meeting; the second is to follow the above steps **except** bring the proposal with you to the meeting. You will have to do what works best for you and best suits your own operating style. If you send it before your appointment, keep it brief and to the point. You can bring all the support documentation (clippings, articles, collateral material, etc.) with you. And, as with any sales call, always reconfirm just prior to your meeting to ensure that the time is still available to properly present your event.

There are several ways to do in-person presentations, from the simple typed proposal to a complete presentation including video, slides, and other presentation materials and, of course, Powerpoint. Often event salespeople think the more sponsorship dollars being requested the larger the presentation. Not necessarily true. Remember, sponsors are interested in how your event can enhance their marketing objectives and, in most cases, increase sales. If your presentation is factual, concise, targeted to their needs, and provides a great return on the investment, you can do a simple pocket-folder presentation with typed sheets. Content is more important than form.

Of course, good selling techniques are also needed. "No" usually means "Not yet," "I need more information," "You haven't listened to my needs," etc.

After the meeting, whether or not the call has resulted in a sale, make sure you follow up with a thank-you note. In addition, if they have declined to participate, stay in communication with them through press releases, monthly updates on your progress, invitations to activities within your event, etc. By keeping them apprised of your activities you might find them more receptive to sponsoring next year!

Chapter 36 – HOW TO SELL FIRST-TIME EVENTS

Sponsorship sales for a first-time event are difficult. There's neither a track record nor past experience for the event, so all you have to sell is estimated attendance, exposure and marketing opportunities. How can you make your sponsorship offering so attractive that companies will be willing to make the investment and the commitment? By enhancing it with media and on-site tangibles that have value, even without the event.

The first step in selling your "new" event is the same as for an established event: analyze your event from the standpoint of who will be attending and who will be participating. What are the demographics and psychographics of these two potential audiences? What is the anticipated attendance/participation? Make a realistic estimate of the numbers involved. This information will be invaluable later on in helping you decide which sponsors to target for participation in this event as well as providing them with valuable information to help in the decision-making process.

After determining the potential audience, start negotiating for your media partners, selecting those whose demographics and psychographics most closely match those of your event. These partners can be radio, television, cable, newspapers and/or magazines. Initially you may have to offer them a more prominent sponsorship in return for the media allocations. Do whatever is necessary to ensure that you have a marketable package. The media package you negotiate must give you a certain number of advertising pages if it is print, and a certain number of commercials if it is the electronic media (radio, TV, cable). In addition, you want to have the editorial coverage defined and committed as part of the total sponsorship package.

Now, you have your event and your media partners. You have defined your event's audience(s) and have a good profile of attendees and participants. Start researching potential sponsors by looking for those companies that want the consumers your event will attract. You can find this information by studying annual reports, reading trade publications, researching the company and/or its products, looking at their marketing materials, analyzing their media placements, and even talking with people within the organizations you are targeting. Do this for at least two dozen companies. This upfront research time is invaluable since it will help you clearly define your most logical sponsorship candidates for your first-time event.

You've analyzed your event, you've aligned yourself with media partners and you've done your homework on potential sponsors. Now it's time to prepare your sponsorship proposals. Your company research has already helped you understand your target sponsors' marketing strategies. Keep those in mind when you prepare your sponsorship offering. Be sure to offer a mix of elements that includes media, hospitality, on-site participation, sales promotion, and VIP privileges. Keep in mind the research you did on the sponsors and address how those specific needs can be met through participation in your event. **Customize each proposal and make a preliminary contact with each potential sponsor before sending the sponsorship package.** Never mass-produce your sponsorship packages and never send generic, mass mailings soliciting sponsorship. That's a very expensive way to solicit sponsors and seldom does it give you a high return on your time and materials investment.

Of course, the best way to sell any event is through the personal sales call. In this way you are present to overcome any objections, answer any and all questions, provide additional insight into the event possibly not covered by your proposal, and deal with the myriad of issues that are part of any sponsorship negotiation.

And, be prepared to negotiate. Many people in the position to negotiate sponsorship contracts treat sponsorship like buying antiques or a used car. Whatever the asking price, they are going to try to get more by paying less. Be prepared for these tactics and know what you can afford to do without sacrificing the quality or integrity of your event. And, remember, although this is a first-time event, if it is successful the sponsors will expect similar terms next year! Don't offer such bargain basement prices that you can't recover for next year's negotiations. Or, if you find you are taking less than you feel is fair, get a sponsorship commitment for two or three years, using an escalating scale based on first-year results and performance.

Many first-time event objections can be overcome if you come to the meeting prepared. Study other first-time events to determine how effectively they met their sponsorship commitments. Be prepared to present that information on your sponsorship sales call. Get testimonial letters from first-time event sponsors defining the value of their participation and how their association has grown through involvement with a first-time event. A strong selling point with a first-time event is the ability for a sponsor to get involved at the beginning with the positive benefits of growing with the event.

Of course, when the event is a success and you have delivered all you promised … and more … the renewal of existing sponsors and addition of new sponsors will be easier than the first year. However, it's not as much fun or as exciting as that very first sponsorship sale for a first-time event!

Chapter 37 – MANAGING SPONSORSHIP ON SITE FOR GUARANTEED RENEWALS

Without sponsors we wouldn't have events! Recognizing that, let's look at what we can do to keep sponsors happy with their participation and to make sure they renew for future events.

Of course, when you enter into a sponsorship arrangement you will have a contract. Within that contract will be spelled out the various elements that comprise the sponsorship package. The more detailed this listing can be, the easier it is for sponsors and event producers alike to manage the sponsorship.

Once you have the complete listing of sponsorship benefits, make sure the sponsoring organization assigns someone from that company to follow through on these benefits. **Don't let sponsors hand you a check and take a "hands-off" approach to their participation. If you do, you are doomed to failure.**

In addition to providing sponsorship dollars, the sponsoring organization should attempt to integrate their sponsorship into their other marketing efforts to enhance their participation. This means including the event representative in the marketing planning process as well as involving other departments within the sponsoring organization. All the players should become familiar with the terms of sponsorship to prevent any misunderstandings or miscommunications. Make sure both the event and the sponsoring organization have assigned a single contact who is responsible for the sponsorship management and implementation.

Working together, go through the contract and make up the complete list of sponsorship benefits into a checklist that you can work from when organizing and producing the event. Then, work to that list. For example, if the sponsor is promised four 3' x 10' banners, and the locations have been specifically designated, don't cut corners and only put up three or make them a different size.

Incidentally, whenever making up graphics for the client, be sure to request the corporate logo identity graphic standards manual. The graphic standards manual will tell you where to place the logo, which PMS colors to use, its placement in relation to other logos, where and when the logo can and cannot be used, etc. Don't make any assumptions about corporate logos. Huge sums of money have been invested in the standards and you are expected to honor the criteria established for the treatment of that logo. A very large sponsorship can be lost over what you might perceive to be a simple misinterpretation of the corporate logo. To the sponsoring organization, the logo is sacred -- treat it accordingly. Make sure all graphics material that contains the corporate logo(s) is approved by the sponsoring organization(s). With today's technology, that's easy. Just fax or e-mail the material to them, get a signature, and have it returned to you..

During the event setup, make sure your sponsor on-site liaison comes to the site and approves location and placement, as stated in the contract, of the various elements …

banners, signs, hospitality, etc. If, for some extraordinary reason, that person is not available, take photos to include in the post-event report. As expressed earlier, ideally, the sponsor will have assigned both an internal liaison as well as an on-site sponsor representative who attends the event and makes sure the sponsor rights and benefits are provided by the event.

The post-event report is a wrap-up of the event and contains attendance figures, weather report, photos of the event and activities within that event, media coverage, recap of events, and summary of sponsorship benefits provided. This should be provided to the client no later than 30 days after the event.

If you have lived up to your commitment, the renewal should be virtually automatic and the relationship solidified for future projects.

Chapter 38 – MEASURING AND REPORTING RESULTS

All event-related programs need to be measured in order to improve the ROI for both the sponsoring company and the organizer. From the event organizers point-of-view, we strongly suggest using the post-event report, which is a summary of all promotional and marketing activity plus the value of that activity. Sponsors may want to undertake their own measurements to augment this effort. Using traditional qualitative and quantitative research for pre- and post-analysis, you can measure awareness, attitudes and perceptions. Add broadcast delivery, publicity and sales results and you should have a reasonable understanding of how effective the programs were. Equally important, but more difficult to measure, is the impact the event has on customer relationships. However, by establishing pre-event criteria for measurement based on past sales results, you can develop a good form of measurement and evaluation.

There are four main steps in the measurement process:

- First, identify internal and external resources;

- Second, develop the measurement plan itself -- its methodology, timing, cost and deliverables;

- Third, clearly identify the decisions to be made with the results -- refer back to the primary expectations of the sponsors;

- Fourth, identify who needs the results, why, and when.

When using a combination of internal and external researchers, be sure each knows what their roles and responsibilities are and, to the extent possible, be sure they understand event marketing. The quality of their analysis will depend on not only how well they know their trade, but also how much they know about measuring events.

What Decisions Will Be Made as a Result of the Research?

Usually every measurement plan is driven by the need to make one or more of the following decisions:

- Can the event be improved?

- Can the market programs produce better results?

- Do you want to continue sponsoring the event?

- If you continue sponsoring the event, do you want to change your sponsorship position?

Some of the areas you may want to evaluate and possibly improve include:

- Presence and visibility at the event;

- Community and public relations;

- Product sampling;
- Customer hospitality experience;
- Product image;
- Product sales;
- Market share;
- Communication of product/service attributes;
- Brand awareness;
- Distribution levels;
- New distribution channels;
- Links with opinion leaders;
- Employee morale;
- Media coverage;
- Other sponsor funding;
- Ticket revenue;
- Merchandise royalties;
- Television revenue.

For those of you selling sponsorships, this list is an indication of what sponsors are looking for in their sponsorship partnerships. Consider them when putting together a proposal for participation.

Chapter 39 – DEVELOPING THE POST-EVENT REPORT

Your event is over. The last tent is gone, the grounds are cleaned up, the last food vendor has left, your sponsors were happy ... you're done! Or, so you think. However, you still have work to do.

Always provide your sponsors with a post-event report. You will have maintained a good close working relationship with your sponsors during the pre-event and at the event process. You were meticulous about writing a contract that properly outlined all the various rights and benefits associated with the sponsorship. Your organization worked closely with the sponsor's representatives, on-site, to ensure that all contractual obligations (and more!) were met. Now, you need to report back to the sponsor.

Remember the old presentation saying ... "Tell them what you are going to tell them; tell them; then tell them what you told them"? The latter part of that statement refers to the post-event evaluation report.

Hopefully, during the event, you took lots of pictures, particularly pictures of crowds, signs, banners, tents ... anything that demonstrated that people were there and that the sponsors' logos and other branded materials had high visibility and exposure.

Keep samples of all printed materials ... tickets, site maps, program books, press releases, newspaper and magazine clippings (with sponsor's names), posters, flyers, branded merchandise (T-shirts, hats, coolies, etc.), sample of in-store promotions, samples of coupons or bouncebacks, samples of entry forms ... make sure you have enough of these materials for all sponsors for your post-event report.

Next, summarize all the component parts of your sport/event. This includes total attendance (and profile of attendees, when possible ... kids, parents, teens, etc.), summary of media exposure (radio and TV will provide you with a notarized log of the times and dates when your commercials/ promotions ran; newspapers and magazines will send you tear sheets), how many posters and flyers were distributed and in what geographic areas, how many banners were hung and where, the number of audio announcements made (sample script, too) and how many times each sponsor's name was mentioned, number of contest/promotion entries (database development, etc.), number of coupons or bouncebacks distributed ... in short, anything that had a sponsor's name on it or gave sponsor exposure.

Now, put it into a list and attach a value/price to the component parts. The media will be easy since the summary report will have a value attached to it. The tougher part is attaching a value to some of the components such as banner exposure, ticket stub exposure, audio announcements, etc. However, here are some simple estimates to use in providing your sponsors with a post-event evaluation of their investment. The two elements that must be included are dollar value and number of exposures:

1. For banners and signage at the event, contact The Traffic Audit Bureau for Media Measurement, 212-972-8075 and get them to help you evaluate the value. If you want

to use a "straw man" figure, use $100 per 1,000 people that see the sign. Therefore, if you have an event that attracts 10,000 people, the value of the signage exposure is $1,000 per sign. For banners and signage that are put up **before** the event, contact your local Department of Transportation (DOT) to get traffic counts (cars/pedestrians) and then use the same media measurement that you used for the event exposure.

2. For the media (radio/TV/print) break out each sponsor's exposure (were they all mentioned in all the spots or did you divide the campaign and give each sponsor a selected number of exposures) and use the media's evaluation. Then, get the media to tell you how many people those messages reached (circulation for newspapers and magazines, listeners for radio, viewers for TV) and include those exposure numbers.

3. For branded merchandise, tickets, hospitality, etc. break out the same way ... number of exposures and dollar value. (SEE CHAPTER 11, "How to Price Your Event Components")

When preparing your post-event report, use a three-column report (going left to right) with the following three headings:

- Column 1 (Sponsor components) ... banners, tickets, media, etc.;

- Column 2 (Number of impressions) ... listeners, attendance, viewers, etc.;

- Column 3 (Dollar value) ... tickets, value of media, banner expense, etc.

Then, just total the columns! This post-event report should be delivered within 30 days after the completion of your event. Hopefully, you will have under-promised and over-delivered, showing a minimum return on investment of 3:1. (See sample post-event report in Appendix C)

What is the bonus value of the post-event report? Besides letting the sponsor understand the full value of the sponsorship, it's a terrific sales tool for renewal or extension of the sponsorship.

Chapter 40 – EVALUATING CAUSE MARKETING: A STRATEGIC APPROACH EXISTS

Cause-Related Marketing (CRM) is a growing trend as corporations are discovering that what's good for the community is also good for business. Cause marketing ties a company's charitable contributions to the sale of products and services in order to increase consumer awareness and company image.

Organized to increase the bottom line, business sponsorship has gone from approximately 1,000 companies spending $450 million in 1984 to 25,000+ companies spending over one billion dollars in 2004. Cause marketing will continue to increase as more and more companies seek non-traditional methods of supporting products. Is cause marketing suited for every corporation? Maybe. The key is to understand what you are trying to achieve with your program, and to maintain a positive relationship and understanding of the charity you are working with.

Every company and non-profit organization will develop its own format for choosing and evaluating a cause marketing program, but the following gives some introductory guidelines:

- **Good company citizenship is good business**. It has been proven time and again that those companies exhibiting conscience are consistently the most successful. The recent Cone/Roper Benchmark Survey found that 80 percent of all people questioned expressed the importance of buying from companies that make charitable contributions.

- **Check references**. Corporations and charities should check each other out with the same due diligence as hiring a new employee. Corporations need to analyze how a charity spends its money, and they should talk with other corporations who have worked with the charity to determine its credibility. Charities need to take the time to study a corporation to determine its reputation in the community.

- **Target audience**. A successful cause marketing campaign must match the cause to the desired target audience of a corporation. An alcohol company would typically not look towards a children's charity; obviously neither would a tobacco company.

- **Lead time**. One of the most important elements of a successful CRM program effort is lead time. Packaged goods manufacturers were some of the first to use cause marketing, and have reaped the most benefits, in part because they have more time to work on a campaign than other corporations.

- **Timing**. The timing of the program itself is important. Companies often try CRM when sales are low. This type of approach almost always fails. The best programs should not be run in the best months or worst months for a company. Somewhere in-between is the best.

- **Involve employees**. The best CRM programs are team efforts that involve all levels of employees. When the CEO of a corporation stands shoulder-to-shoulder with employees in a program, it makes for a winner.

- **State your goals**. Don't just announce a cause-related tie-in. Say what it's for. The promotional message should state the amount of money trying to be raised, and what it will be used for. This will help people identify with, and develop empathy for, the cause.

- **Dominate a cause**. Corporations will see the most benefit if they can be the pre-eminent benefactor. If you are splitting your efforts among several charitable organizations, you tend to lose exposure.

Cause marketing is here to stay. As with all marketing, the corporations that are successful with it will be the ones that take the time to understand it, evaluate it, and improve upon it. Unfortunately, like so many other marketing strategies, "cause marketing" has become a buzzword that many non-profits and corporations toss around, but have no idea how to incorporate into their plans. A successful cause marketing program must create a "win-win" situation for both the corporation and the non-profit.

The standard for a successful CRM program was set over 20 years ago with the joint restoration committee for the Statue of Liberty. During a three-month period in 1983, American Express donated one cent for each transaction on its American Express Card. This program resulted in a $1.7 million donation to the restoration of the Statue of Liberty and increased the use of the card by over 20 percent. This is a classic example of a true "win-win" program.

Many non-profits continue to view cause marketing as a simple donation to a charity without understanding that the corporation must benefit. Corporations have also tried to shy away from their responsibility by soliciting programs that use a charity's name, but don't deliver solid financial rewards to the non-profit.

Cause-Related Marketing is a tested winner and has earned exceptional marketing results for corporations but, as with any strategy, it needs to be done with the right resources and the proper thought process.

Chapter 41 – HOW TO ENHANCE YOUR EVENT PARTICIPATION AS A NON-PROFIT

As a beneficiary of an existing event, you have the same rights as any of the participating sponsors. This includes all media coverage, signage, prominence on all collateral material, and inclusion in all marketing efforts. Make sure your organization's logo is included in all signage, on the merchandise (T-shirts, hats, etc.), and during the event. In fact, you should enter into a sponsorship contract, just as the other sponsors have for the event, that spells out exactly what your organization and the event expect of each other. To facilitate this discussion, the following checklist outlines those items to be discussed with the event organizers. (This process is not necessary when you own the event but is vital when you are part of an existing event):

Non-Profit Rights

1. Signage:
   - Logo placement on signage;
   - Approval of logo usage/placement;
   - Number of signs with your logo;
   - Signage placement at event;
   - Pre-event signage.
2. Advertising credits:
   - Logo placement in advertising;
   - Approval of logo usage/placement;
   - Advertising placement;
   - Pre-event advertising.
3. Merchandising rights:
   - Logo placement on merchandise;
   - Approval of logo usage/placement;
   - Revenue sharing from sales.
4. Public relations rights:
   - Logo placement on media releases;
   - Approval of logo usage/placement;
   - Approval of your organization's involvement in event;
   - Right to distribute media releases through your organization's media list.
5. Benefits:
   - Pre-event appearances;
   - On-site participation;
   - Revenue for the non-profit;
   - Visibility at event functions;
   - Public acknowledgment of participation;
   - Non-profit employee hospitality;
   - Donor hospitality.
6. Future options:
   - Right of first refusal for following year;

91

- Cancellation terms;
- Increased revenue benefits.
7. Indemnification/liability:
   - Hold harmless clause;
   - Insurance protection;
   - Errors and omission protection;
   - Force majeure, rain date.
8. Non-Disclosure:
   - Contract confidentiality;
   - Control information for public knowledge.

By using this checklist for contract negotiations, you can protect your organization from negative public relations and assure your organization of fair and equitable treatment by the event organizers.

Chapter 42 – HOW SPONSORS CAN MAXIMIZE A NON-PROFIT SPONSORSHIP

Huge corporations and large companies have been sponsoring non-profit organizations or events for years. Corporate philanthropy is a strategic tool that should not be overlooked by small businesses and organizations. In addition to strengthening or creating a positive image, not to mention the tax break, this tactic increases employee and customer loyalty.

Cause-Related Marketing (CRM) is a new trend that links sponsorship to increases in profits and sales. Companies tie their name and products directly to a specific cause. Since repeat buyers are often crucial to a small businesses' success, and since the current consumer wants to patronize socially conscious companies and organizations, CRM is an imaginative device to create customer loyalty.

For small businesses or organizations, there are a few guidelines to observe when making a sponsorship decision and negotiating a deal. From a public relations standpoint, each one should be evaluated to justify the expense of endorsing a campaign.

Before hooking up with a program or event, analyze why this particular combination would be a good association for your company. Analyze what positive impact will result from this connection. Consider the goodwill factor, whether the cause or event has a similar target audience (demographics) and how the public can identify your company with the cause or event. Conversely, do not try to link your company and its mission with a cause that would be inappropriate. For instance, if your company makes diet pills, do not consider sponsoring a campaign to wipe out anorexia in young girls. For sponsorship to be effective, the public must retain a positive mental association between the cause and your company - don't make the leap too difficult.

In addition to giving money, companies or associations also benefit by donating their products or services to a cause. A baked goods company can give breads and rolls to the local food bank, a construction company executive can teach low-cost remodeling skills to low-income homeowners, or a public relations firm could donate its services to publicize an event to raise money for the construction of a new hospital wing to treat pediatric cardiology patients.

Determine whether your company or organization will be the only sponsor. If other companies will also be sponsors, evaluate the possibility of conflicts with your business interests. The consumer may link your company and products or services with the reputation of other corporate sponsors.

Request that press conferences publicizing the upcoming event be held at your office or place of business. Additionally, request that your company logo be printed on all published materials for the sponsored event or program. This will increase consumer awareness and enhance your corporate image.

Ascertain the possibility of entertaining your clients and distributing company promotional materials at sponsored events. If the occasion is a celebrity event, inquire if your company may have access to the celebrity for promotional or public relations purposes. Ask that the organizer mention your sponsorship in press releases and public service announcements. Request permission to distribute your own press releases regarding your sponsorship to the media and your industry's trade publications.

As you can see, the benefits of negotiating a sponsorship with charities or other affiliations are obvious. Consumers will appreciate your sense of social responsibility. This, in turn, leads to better customer relations and an enhanced corporate image, giving your organization the competitive edge!

By using careful consideration when choosing a sponsorship that fits the needs of the sponsor (your company or organization) and the needs of those sponsored (the cause), you can generate a stronger and more loyal relationship with your employees and customers. You have a winning combination.

Chapter 43 – HOW TO RESEARCH GRANTS ON THE WEB

The Internet had been characterized by grantseekers as both a magic bullet and a bottomless well of endless information and frustration. By overcoming any anxieties you may have about "going online," while learning to harness the 'Net' to your own advantage, you can maximize your knowledge while drastically reducing the time and effort you used to spend tracking down traditional print-based sources of funding information. However, as the Internet becomes a bigger and better source of grant leads, a number of cautions loom like blinking traffic lights. Ignore them and you will be destined not only for hours of flailing about from Web site to Web site, but for receipt of as many proposal rejections as your organization experienced **before** the Internet was discovered by grantseekers! In short, you must view the Internet as a convenient and fun beginning to your grant search - a useful tool which should not and cannot replace the "old" media (e.g., foundation and corporate directories, funder program guidelines, government RFPs [requests for proposals], or phone and in-person conversations with program officers).

While funders and nonprofits alike have become excited about the speed and ease with which information can be located and exchanged, the Internet's limitations as a grantseeker's panacea must be recognized. Some examples will help you keep things in perspective:

1. The number of foundation and corporate grantmakers with Web pages is rising as more and more of the country's 40,000+ foundations discover the value of web access;

2. Information of federal grant opportunities is still scattered throughout the 'Net, and the way leads and data are presented varies widely from agency to agency. Meanwhile, individual states lag far behind the federal government in posting opportunities electronically;

3. There is tremendous duplication and confusion, as a growing number of online indexes, "catalogs," personal Web pages, and "alerts" link to identical and overlapping sites;

4. Unless you are reading the funder's "own words" (meaning, their own Web page), there is a good chance that the person designing the summary has omitted certain critical information (such as specific program priorities, geographic and other restrictions, and the preferred initial contact required by the funder) in the interest of creating a speedy or snappy presentation.

Despite the growing attempt at "user friendliness" and accessibility projected by Worldwide Web pages, very little has changed behind the scenes in the grantmakers' world. Private and public funders still: a) demand that their application guidelines or RFP's be digested fully and carefully, and that all proposals respond clearly to each specific requirement; and b) refuse, in most cases, to meet or talk at length with applicants, or to accept full proposals - unless they (the grantmakers) initiate the contact.

Many funders complain that the Internet is actually increasing the overload of poorly written and inappropriately-targeted proposals, as grantseekers give in to the easy temptation to "cut and paste" and to mass-market the same proposal to any funder whose program is summarized (often incorrectly) somewhere on the 'Net.

For those just starting out, investing some learning time upfront will save you hours of thrashing around, down the road. Here are some tips for making your trips through the Internet more efficient and more rewarding - and more likely to result in grants:

1. If you are an Internet beginner, try to attend a "hands-on" workshop or seminar - but don't leave until the leader takes you through the steps of actually locating a Web page, or answers all the questions you have. Though the sites demonstrated may not be relevant to nonprofit agencies, the "how to's" for locating them and taking the best advantage of their content are the same for everyone;

2. Some of the larger home pages for nonprofits have an extensive "Help" or learning section. There are also increasing numbers of FAQs (frequently asked questions) pages on all aspects of nonprofit management and fundraising that are linked to major Web pages. Spend a few hours investing in your own online education - it's free, and you don't have to leave your home or office!;

3. Never hesitate to consult a young person if you need an answer or shortcut, or if you find yourself just plain "stuck." Kids thrive on technology and are free of the anxiety that plagues many adult learners. And always listen to a child who claims to know a faster, easier, or "better" way to do something - they probably do!;

4. Often the best sites are those recommended by colleagues - even cybercolleagues! Scan print and online trade publications for recommended Web sites, listservs to join, and new search engines or other services.

The fastest way to develop a tension headache, dizziness, and pounding heart is to devote several hours to frantic net-surfing, then realize you've discovered practically nothing of any real use - and you won't be able to find it again, anyway! The keys here are **discipline** and **focus.**

1. Set a time limit - maximum two hours - for your initial voyages. Take frequent, but short, "stretch breaks";

2. Begin with the general and work toward the more specific. (E.g., "I'm going to start by exploring sites on the subject of elementary education in the U.S. Then I'll focus in on sites concerning math, science and technology. Then I'll search for ones with information on funding in those various subject areas.) Though your eye may be caught by sites on pre-school research from the UK, the president's views on technology in education, or students' letters to other children surviving a major disaster, reign in your impulses, and visit those other sites on another day;

3.   Identify a few major sites (such as the Foundation Center's home page, at http://fdncenter.org) which you feel comfortable using and which have easily-located links to subjects and sites that you will want to return to visit often. Include a few "mega-indexes," "catalogs" or directories for nonprofits (you will find ones ranging from Alzheimer's to Environmental Organizations to Youth and Families.) Many such links can be found through the home pages of The Foundation Center, The Grantsmanship Center (http://www.tgci.com) or the popular search engine Yahoo (http://www.yahoo.com);

4.   Whenever you find a home page to which you would like to return - or, more importantly, a useful but remote link or sub-sub page buried with a page - bookmark it immediately, to spare yourself having to write down and later type in repeatedly its long URL (Web address). With some practice, you can arrange your bookmark table of contents in a logical order and in groupings by subject.

Some of the best sources of information on the Internet are not - or are more than - traditional "home pages." These include listservs (or mailing lists), newsgroups and discussions, online journals, and a variety of "alerts." These media can provide you with not only the most up-to-date information, but also a host of colleagues from around the country and the world. *But you must use them judiciously, or you will find yourself misinformed or perhaps **over-informed***, feeling like you're drowning in unstoppable waves of data.

Don't sign up for every wonderful-sounding listserv, free e-mail publication or "alert," or your will find yourself spending literally hours of each day weeding through messages which clog up your electronic mailbox, only a minority of which will prove of use to you. Consult colleagues or respected trade publications for recommendations. And **always** remember to save the instructions for **unsubscribing** and **subscribing** on paper or to your hard drive, so that you can get off an unproductive list or temporarily stop delivery while you're on vacation.

There are some wonderful online magazines for grantseekers, including The Foundation Center's Philanthropy Digest, Philanthropy Journal (http://www.philanthropy-journal.org), and the magazine of The Grantsmanship Center. These are constantly improving and changing, while new online publications are appearing all the time. Bookmark the most appealing, and make it a point to visit them weekly for the latest "how-to's" for fund raising, as well as news on grant opportunities, workshops and conferences, government funding initiatives, and major changes in the foundation world.

Online journals are becoming increasingly powerful, allowing you to search back issues, participate in online discussions, and link instantly to other resources. Bear two things in mind, however, to temper your excitement: a) as with print publications, the grant "news" you receive is being received simultaneously by thousands of other grantseekers; and b) "digested" information may come to you faster electronically, but it is still a distillation which may omit many important details, such as grant restrictions, deadlines, and correct contact information.

Regardless of the online source you are using on a particular funder or grant opportunity - a Worldwide Web homepage, an "annotated" link (often a paragraph-long summary), an announcement of a government initiative, a memo passed along from listserv to listserv - you will need to compile the same basic data before you can even begin considering applying for a grant. If the electronic source leaves "holes" in the picture, you will need to augment the profile with information from other Internet sites on this funder or grant, or to fill in the missing pieces by consulting:

a) One of The Foundation Center or The Taft Group's major directories on foundations, corporations, or grants in specific fields;

b) These organizations' databases, which are now available on CD-ROM;

c) The funder's own program guidelines, annual report, or RFP; or

d) The organization's 990 PF (IRS tax return filed by private foundations).

Now that you're ready to start surfing, two "tips" will help reduce the number of error messages (which often cause new and veteran Web surfers alike to pull out their hair):

1. Perfect typing is of paramount importance! A seemingly insignificant error (e.g., transposition of a period (.) and a slash(/) or a single missed letter will result in a "could not retrieve" or other non-informative error message! When this occurs, your first response should be to simply erase and re-type the address; if this does not produce the Web page, consult the source from which you got the address; and if *this* doesn't work....

2. Sometimes a "could not retrieve" or similar message means that a site is receiving too much "traffic" at that moment, is temporarily "under construction," or that the server (or sites, such as The Foundation Center's home page and those of various federal agencies (ending in ".gov") are frequently unreachable; simply try later that day, or the next day at a different time.

So, as you explore grant searching through the Internet you can avoid feeling overwhelmed while increasing your efficiency if you remember to:

1. **Stay focused on your goal;**

2. **Break whenever you start to feel frustrated or confused;**

3. **Consult other sources to flesh out information gleaned from the 'Net';**

4. **Have fun!**

Chapter 44 – SPONSORSHIP AND FUNDRAISING ... WHAT'S THE DIFFERENCE?

As more and more non-profits discover that fundraising isn't giving them a sufficient return they are considering alternative ways of generating revenue for their particular cause. One of the ways available to them is sponsorship. But, what is sponsorship and how does it differ from fundraising?

First ...

The term "fund-raiser" is primarily used by non-profit organizations and, more specifically, those designated as 501(c)3 by the internal revenue service. Seldom will you find a fund-raiser in a for profit organization. This term is used when a donation is made and there is no marketing value as a result of the donation.

Second ...

Sponsorship is used primarily when discussing money invested in an event, an activity, an organization that has some form of payback whether it be improved media relations, enhanced sales, increased product visibility, or any of a number of marketing components that enhance the sponsoring organization's marketing efforts.

Third ... and last

The goals are the same ... to raise money. The target companies are the same ... the contact people in those companies are totally different. The approach, strategies and tactics are totally different. Here's a brief look at each and a summary of the respective approaches...

Fundraising

Both the mindset and process contrast sharply with the sponsorship approach. For fundraising, using the medium of direct marketing (direct mail, telemarketing or the internet), the fundraiser puts together an "appeal" --asking for money -- and then sends it out to a target audience. There is no direct one-on-one selling and the fundraiser is apologetic for his/her approach. The primary benefit to a company giving a donation to a fundraiser, besides helping a worthy cause, is the tax deductibility of the contribution.

Sponsorship

Conversely, for sponsorship, the approach is highly targeted where sponsor wants and needs are matched carefully to event/organization opportunities so both sides benefit. The sponsorship salesperson meets with the sponsor and discusses the benefits to be realized from sponsorship and works with that sponsor on cross promotions, exposure and measurement criteria. The benefit to the company investing in a sponsorship is mutually decided between the sponsorship company and sponsored organization. This could be increased sales, enhanced product exposure, improved employee relations, etc., etc., etc.

Summary

Which one offers more? They both have value and, if combined, offer a sponsor the synergy of being associated with a worthwhile cause (Cause-Related Marketing-CRM) and a marketing investment that provides a measurable return. The convergence of fundraising and sponsorship is win/win for **all** parties involved.

Chapter 45 – How to Work with Corporations: Marketing vs. Philanthropic Donations

According to the Internal Revenue Service, corporations may give up to 10% of their pre-tax income in tax-deductible donations. However, most large businesses give away only about 1% of their pre-tax dollars. Unless corporations have a separately endowed foundation giving is very closely tied to profits and if a corporation does not make a profit one year, giving may drop sharply the next.

The Three Corporate Funding Doors

Unfortunately, the majority of nonprofits don't know how to ask corporations for money. They approach them in the same way they approach foundations and government, and this is a mistake. To raise money from a corporation, you need to think like one.

Think of a corporation as having three doors for nonprofits to enter when they seek assistance. The *first door* is called **"Membership"**. This is a very small door around the side of the building where the corporation sets aside a small amount of money to join chambers of commerce, trade associations, and civic groups such as the Lions and Rotary. Corporate membership contributions are generally in the $100-500 range. If you have a membership program or can develop a corporate category within an overall donor program, this is a good way to get on the corporate radar screen.

The *second door*, toward the front of the building, is the **"Philanthropy"** entrance. This is the traditional door, used by the majority of nonprofit organizations. Corporate grants are usually in the $1,000-10,000 range and are given on a year-to-year basis. The corporate giving staff is frequently housed in the public relations department (a tip off to the next level of funding) and their goal is to spread the limited philanthropic dollars over a large number of organizations. Corporations like their employees to be involved in the giving process, and so a corporate person on your board or a committee can be instrumental in securing continued or long-term funding for your group.

If the corporation does not have a presence in your community, the chances of receiving support are minimal. However, although companies in your community are always the best bet, be on the lookout for corporations that will be moving to your area or that are planning to buy out an existing company. They want some quick visibility and this is an excellent opportunity to get your organization's message across before they arrive and you must compete with all the other groups. The health care and banking industries are prime examples of a rapidly changing business climate where companies look to build a corporate identity and community acceptance as quickly as possible.

Don't forget that companies of all sizes are excellent places to obtain donated office equipment, food and supplies, volunteers and technical experts. Small local businesses are often overlooked, but when every dollar counts, explore your options for free food at board meetings, printing and copying, or flowers for your special event.

The *third door*, right at the front of the building, is the **"Marketing"** entrance. Corporations spend billions of dollars every year to market their good and services and if your nonprofit can assist the company to enhance its image, reach potential customers, or reinforce existing customer relationships, they will want to work with you. And, besides, it's good business for corporations to tax shelter their marketing dollars through your organization.

During the past decade, the majority of corporate dollars going to nonprofit groups have come from the marketing rather than philanthropic budgets. In Cause-Related Marketing, the relationship moves from that of grantor-grantee to one of partnering in projects to benefit both the company and the nonprofit. Bill Shore, director of Share Our Strength and author of *Revolution of the Heart,* was a leader in this technique in the 1980s with Charge Against Hunger, a partnership with American Express. Now we see it everywhere.

What are companies looking for? Usually, most companies want to promote the image of:

- **A friendly and caring corporate citizen responding to critical community needs** (corporations are becoming heavily involved in high risk youth and education issues);

- **A protector of the environment** ("dolphin-friendly" tuna and "save the rain forest" products are overflowing from supermarket shelves);

- **A company that treats its employees well** (day care and elder care concerns are moving to the top of many corporate agendas).

What does it take for a nonprofit to raise money through Cause-Related Marketing? A bit of chutzpah, a basic understanding of what the corporation and your nonprofit are looking for, some confidence, and a real desire to move the relationship into a true partnership. Put yourself inside the mind of the marketing director who is asking, "What can this organization do for me?" If you can figure out a way to help the company get in front of customers, while generating resources for your nonprofit, you have a win-win situation.

Can't think of where to start? Pull together a group of your stakeholders for a creative session and let the ideas flow freely. Think of all the possible corporations within your area and all the possible projects you might work on together. Some ideas to get you started include:

- A publication or service that meets the needs of your constituents and the corporation's customers - a traffic safety group might obtain corporate sponsorship from an insurance company;

- A needed service for the corporation's employees - a counseling center might negotiate an Employee Assistance Program contract to provide counseling services;

- Help corporations to comply with the law - a disability group might market its "accessibility audit" services;

- Get your message across to the public in a well-traveled corporate thoroughfare - an arts group might obtain sponsorship for a display in a corporate lobby. (This works just as well for human service groups.);

- Persuade a supermarket to devote a certain percentage of its sales to your group on a given day - then increase sales by mobilizing your supporters to shop in that store.

When you have lots of possibilities, you can begin to narrow the focus and pick one or two corporations to approach.

It's best to start with companies where you already have a relationship or where you have someone who can introduce you to a senior executive. Look to the bank where you have your account or the company where a number of your volunteers are employed. Sometimes, you may decide to look at companies where you will become a customer. If you decide to shift your bank account, use the opportunity to negotiate for a new line of credit or a reduction in service charges.

When you have identified a likely prospect, find out everything you can about them. Request a copy of their annual report and corporate giving policies, check out the corporation's web page (if they have one), and talk with other people in the community who have had either philanthropic or business dealings with the company.

Developing the Partnership

The next step is to call up the CEO, the marketing director, or any person in the company who is accessible to you, and discuss the possibilities of developing a partnership. Remember that they are looking for visibility, credibility and new customers. As an example, a bank may be interested in marketing its services to the African-American community in your neighborhood. You are a non-profit that works with the African-American community. You may have a small budget, but a lot of credibility with the people you serve. A fairly typical approach would be to ask the bank to sponsor a neighborhood fair.

This is a good start, but it provides a finite sum of money for your nonprofit and only superficial exposure for the bank. Why not offer to follow up the fair by working with the bank over the next year to develop other strategies and opportunities to market their services to your constituency (their potential customers). The difference here is the desire of the nonprofit organization to work with the bank throughout the year on a variety of approaches. In this way, you can educate the company on the needs of your community, they can develop products to suit your constituents, and your nonprofit develops a regular stream of income.

Are there risks in this approach? Sure there are. You would be foolish to think Cause-Related Marketing is a free lunch. It is important to discuss prospective partnerships with your board of directors and other key stakeholders, particularly if you think the partnership might have any negative repercussions with your staff, immediate constituencies, or existing and future funders. Remember that the company will probably be much clearer about its self-interest than you will about yours. This is why it's good to have a few business people on your board of directors to help you evaluate opportunities.

Bear in mind that corporations are one of the principal engines that drive our society. If we want to have long-term support from this funding source, we need to look inside the corporate mindset and ask ourselves how they can support our mission, while we help the business support theirs. In some cases, we just want to ask them to pay a membership fee; in others, we will want a straightforward donation; but for those who want to take the relationship into a partnership, the rewards (and also the risks) can be greater.

Chapter 46 – HOW TO GET STARTED, AS A NON-PROFIT, IN SPONSORSHIP

The easiest way to get started is to become part of an existing event. This gives you an opportunity to observe, firsthand, what is happening and what is needed to have a successful event.

How do you determine the appropriate "fit" for your nonprofit and select a specific event? One easy way, once you have determined those events in which you are interested, is to send the Promoter/Producer Worksheet (see following) to the event organizers and ask them to complete for you. Also, run a credit check on the event organizers to make sure they are part of a legitimate organization and not a fly-by-night group.

PROMOTER/PRODUCER WORKSHEET

I. **BACKGROUND INFORMATION ON** _____(event name)_____

    A. **Company name:** _____

       Address: _____

       City: _____ **State:** _____ **Zip:** _____

       Telephone: (___) _____ **Fax: (___)** _____

       Contact person: _____

       Title: _____

    B. **Other locations (if any):** _____

       _____

    C. **No. of years in business:** _____ **No. of years managing event:** _____

    D. **Other events produced/promoted:** _____

       _____

       _____

    E. **Number of full time staff:** _____

    F. **Names and titles of executives working in this organization including number of years with organization, experience with event and any additional background:**

       1. _____

       _____

       _____

       2. _____

_____

_____

3. _____

_____

_____

G. Any lawsuits pending? Yes ___ No ___ If yes, what are the circumstances?   Please explain:_____

_____

_____

H. Ever declared bankruptcy? Yes ___ No ___ If yes, what are the
   circumstances? Please explain. _____

_____

_____

I. Current sponsor(s): _____

_____

_____

J. Number of years sponsors have been involved: _____

_____

_____

K. Event's insurance coverage (type/dollar amount):

_____

_____

II. EVENT BACKGROUND

A. Name of event: _____

B. Number of years in existence: _____ Initial date: _____

C. Date(s) of event: _____ Length of event: _____

D. What other events occur in the area on the same date as this event?

_____

   Please detail: _____

_____

E. Current title sponsor: _____How long? _____

106

F. Past title sponsor: _____
    Not renewed? _____
    _____

G. List other current sponsors, length of time with event, dollar commit-
    ments: _____
    _____

H. Exact location of event:_____
    _____

I. Event objectives: _____
    _____
    _____

J. Anticipated attendance: _____ Previous year's attendance: _____

K. Composition percentage of attendance per category:

    General public ____% Invited guests ____% Trade ____%

    Press ____% Staff ____% Spouses ____% Other ____%

L. Ticket required? ____ If yes, prepaid or payable at _____

M. Ticket prices and classifications: _____

N. Tax exemption/taxable: _____ Are tickets marked taxed? _____

O. Are tickets torn? ____ Deposit box for stubs? ____

    Prize arrangements? ____ Ticket back promos? ____

P. Re-admission procedure: Hand stamp: ____ Pass: ____ Ticket: ____

    Scanning light: ____ Other: _____

III. NONPROFIT TIE-IN

A. Is there another nonprofit group benefiting from the event? _____
    If yes, name the organization and benefit amount:_____
    _____

B. Any connection between sponsor and beneficiary? _____
    If yes, describe: _____
    _____

C. Are there any specific promotions related to the nonprofit group? ____
    If yes, please detail: _____
    _____

107

D. If you don't have a current nonprofit relationship, are you interested in establishing one? _____ If yes, describe the relationship you are seeking:

_____

_____

IV. EVENT ATTENDANCE/PARTICIPATION PROFILE

A. Describe the event's target audience: _____

_____

_____

B. Is this event unique? _____ If yes, why: _____

_____

C. What is the composition of attendees? (Men, women, children, ages, etc.)

_____

_____

D. Profile the participants:_____

_____

V. MEDIA COVERAGE AND SIGNAGE

A. Is there TV coverage of the event? _____ If yes, cable/network? _____

Is the coverage national, regional, local? _____

Dates and times of airings: _____

Previous year's ratings? _____

B. If televised, is it covered by some third-party measurement?_____

_____

C. What other types of coverage are offered? Radio:_____

Magazines: _____

Newspapers:_____

Other: _____

D. What type of signage is available? (quantity, size, placement): _____

_____

E. Please check all of the following that would be promoting the nonprofit organization's participation in the event:

____ Press kits	____ Schedules
____ Press releases	____ Scoreboards
____ Press conferences	____ Event posters
____ Pre-event publicity tours	____ Ribbons
____ Print interviews	____ Trophies
____ Radio/TV interviews	____ Flags
____ Event brochures	____ Billboards
____ PA announcements	____ Transit
____ Tickets	____ Uniforms
____ Other: _____	

VI. MERCHANDISING AND PROMOTION

A. **What, and how many, of the following items will carry your sponsor?**

____ Hats ____ T-shirts ____ Sweatshirts ____ Pins

____ Balloons ____ Cups/mugs ____ Bags

____ Other _____

_____

B. **Can the organization have a display booth?** _____

Size: _____ Quantity: _____ Restrictions: _____

C. **Can an on-site drawing or contest be conducted?** _____

Are there any restrictions? ____ Please detail: _____

_____

D. **What is the total advertising budget for the event?** _____

E. **How allocated: TV $_____ Number of spots _____**

Stations: _____

Radio $_____ Number of spots _____

Stations: _____

Print $_____ Number of ads _____

Which publications: _____

F. **Programs?** _____ If yes, how many? _____ Ad rates: _____

_____

Distribution: _____

G. Presence at awards presentation? _____

H. Access to athletes/celebrities for special appearances? _____

I. Sales promotion planned:

_____ Contests/sweepstakes	_____ Couponing
_____ Premiums	_____ Sampling
_____ Point of purchase	_____ Incentives

_____ Other _____

J. Other merchandising/promotion/publicity opportunities: _____

_____

VII. CUSTOMER RELATIONS/CORPORATION HOSPITALITY

A. Hospitality opportunities:

_____ Skybox/suite	_____ Parties with celebrities
_____ Exclusive tent area	_____ Food/beverage functions
_____ Priority seating/viewing	_____ Tickets

_____ Other (please detail) _____

B. Are the following provided by the event:

_____ Tents	_____ Tables and chairs
_____ Audio system	_____ Food and beverage
_____ Wait staff	_____ Special event seating
_____ Travel	_____ Accommodations
_____ Welcome gifts	_____ Auto rental

_____ Other: _____

VIII. SECURITY/ON-SITE PROTECTION

A. Is there on-site security? _____

B. Do you have constant on-site communication? _____

C. On-site lost and found? _____

D. Traffic control? _____

E. Medical and safety? _____

To be effective at raising funds through special events, you must approach your participation as you would any other business venture. Here are some very simple rules that will make your participation in an existing event more cost-effective.

DO:

- Take an active part in the event planning and administration;
- Enter into an event contract;
- Follow through with your commitments to the event;
- Protect your organization against any negative publicity;
- Clearly delineate your expectations;
- Enlist the help of your volunteer base.

DON'T:

- Wait until the day of the event to get involved;
- Trust agreements or planning details to memory or vague conversations;
- Make extraordinary demands;
- Expect to reap all the benefits without any effort on your part.

Working in partnership with event management will create a positive relationship that will lead to increased funds for your non-profit organization.

Chapter 47 – CONE/ROPER CAUSE RELATED MARKETING (CRM) TRENDS REPORT

The following are highlights from the latest Cone/Roper Benchmark Survey from a study commissioned by Cone Communications and completed by the Roper Organization. Following are the highlights of this study.

Increased Consumer Acceptance

- Americans are significantly more receptive to CRM than ever before. 88% believe it's acceptable for companies to engage in CRM.

- Cynicism towards CRM is quite low. Only 21% of those surveyed questioned the motives of companies that help good causes.

- Receptivity to CRM is greatest among those most likely to make key purchasing decisions: women 18-49 (84%), parents of young children (81%) and influentials (81%).

Increased Impact

- When price and quality are equal, 90% of consumers would be more likely to switch to a brand associated with a good cause.

- When price and quality are equal, 80% of consumers would be likely to switch to a retail outlet associated with a good cause.

Issues Closest to Home Have Greatest Acceptance

- More than half of those surveyed (59%) want companies to get involved in improving the quality of life on their local level rather than at the national or global.

- Consumers believe companies should take greater steps to deal with the issues of crime (41%), the environment (35%), public education (35%) and poverty (24%). There is a waning interest in companies dealing with the issues of drug abuse, homelessness and substances.

Methodology

Cause-Related Marketing (CRM) is a strategic marketing practice which links a company or its products to a social cause or issue. The goal of CRM is to create enduring bonds and lasting relationships with consumers, employees, retailers, distributors, customers, local communities, and key influencers as well as to enhance brand equity, increases sales, and differentiate parity products in a cluttered marketplace.

Cone Communications is one of the nation's leading marketing public relations firms. For 20+ years, the Boston-based firm has created innovative positions for clients based on their core products, their values, and their customers' critical needs. Roper Starch Worldwide is a well-known New York City-based market research firm.

Chapter 48 – COMMON PROBLEMS OF SPONSOR-SHIP SALES

Whether talking with a group of downtown Main Street managers in Camus, Washington or corporate sponsorship buyers in Toronto, Canada, the problems of sponsorship sales are the same. The following represent some of the most common questions expressed by both buyers and sellers of sponsorship. The first half are expressed by *sellers* of sponsorships; the second half by *buyers* of sponsorships.

Sellers

How do you select an appropriate sponsor for an event?

In order to be effective at sponsorship sales, the event and sponsor must be a good match. In order to determine that, you must know your own event first. What are the demographics of the attendees/participants? (This is simply age, gender, ethnicity, geographic location, education, etc.) What are the psychographics of the attendees/participants? (This is an understanding of their activities, interests and opinions.)

Then, you must understand all the components of your sponsorship offering: What are your media relationships? Do you have signage and other on-site marketing opportunities? What is your total inventory and how is that inventory made available to the sponsor? What is the total exposure that the sponsor (not the event) can realize from participating?

Finally, you must understand the potential sponsors. What do they want? If you have done your homework, studied the annual report, and done a current data search to determine how they are marketing their company/products, you will be able to quickly determine which sponsors would benefit from association with your event and which ones won't. When looking at the available materials, look to see if your event offers the sponsors the types of customers they are looking for. Is the media an enhancement to their current marketing efforts? Do you have something unique in your inventory of "goodies" that will enhance their participation?

Remember, sponsors are bombarded with proposals from thousands of organizations looking for everything from $25 donations to multi-million dollar sponsorships. If you can offer them a marketing environment that helps them achieve their goals (increased sales, increased market share, decreased marketing expense ... these are some of the basics), you have just increased your ability to successfully sell a sponsorship.

How do I find the decision-maker?

First, there's more than one decision-maker for sponsorship. If you consider that sponsorship monies can come from a variety of departments ... advertising, public relations, marketing, employee relations, diversity marketing, even human resources ...

113

you realize that there are a number of options for reaching a number of decision-makers.

You can always ask the "gatekeeper" who the decision-maker is for each of these areas. Of course, if it is a large, publicly held company, you can read the list of officers in the annual report and determine which of them is a decision-maker.

And, last, you can always ask the person you are negotiating with "...is there anyone else that they would like to have involved in the decision-making process." This does not affront the person you are working with and allows them to, comfortably, bring in someone else if that is necessary.

When is an appropriate time to sell a sponsorship?

A "pat" answer would be -- anytime! However, there are some basic rules about timing.

First, you should be starting your sponsorship solicitations a year in advance. Second, you should be sensitive to the budgeting cycles of your potential sponsors. Find out if they work on a calendar year or if their fiscal year is different from the standard January-December time frame. For example, McDonald's fiscal year starts September 1. Since much of their budget planning is done in June, that is the time you would want to schedule a strong sponsorship presentation. If the company works on a calendar year, call and find out when they do their budgeting. Some do it as early as May of the preceding year, others wait until November. In either case, you would want to have material to them before these dates and follow up, closer to the budgeting time, with additional information and strategies for participation.

Buyers

Sellers present too _much_ information.

Be careful of trying to put the Bible on the head of a pin! In your enthusiasm for your property (and you are not alone!), you provide all the information you can think of including all the press clippings, media schedules, program books, collateral material, and whatever else you can think of to get the sponsor excited about participating in your event.

However, what really happens when you provide too much information is that they get bogged down in details and eventually give up since they can't extract the information they need to make an intelligent, informed decision.

Other side of the coin: sellers present too _little_ information.

Just as bad is the person who provides so little information that, again, the sponsor can't make an intelligent, informed decision. If you keep in mind that you are trying to satisfy _sponsor_ needs while still meeting your own, you will present enough material to help them select your event or property for sponsorship.

No follow through after initial contact.

Tenacity is one of the traits of successful sponsorship salespeople. If you have made an initial call and followed up with support material, you have just started the selling process. You need to continue that relationship through telephone calls, in-person visits (where applicable), and consistent follow through. Some sponsorships can be sold in hours ... others take years!

Chapter 49 – GETTING THE SPONSOR TO COMMIT MEANS TAKING A LOOK AT ALTERNATIVES

Corporations have traditionally used sponsorship as mainly image advertising. Evaluations were done simply on the association and how it related to the company. If it was seen as a beneficial association and the money was there, the sponsorship was approved.

Today, many companies, experiencing significant downsizing and budget restraints, are pulling the plug on major sponsorship commitments. On the surface, this may seem like the logical solution but, on further inspection, one realizes that the marketing strategies once achieved through couponing and FSI distribution can now be incorporated into sponsorship and can serve a dual purpose. This not only maximizes a company's expenditures but also allows the savvy brand manager to better capitalize on the events arena.

Let us assume that a company is launching a new product. Traditionally, a major amount of funding would go into the testing and consumer response phase of the launch. If a brand manager were to take a look at the projected target market and research lesser known events that reach that market more specifically, then that same manager could hone in on an excellent win-win situation. If that same manager were to go a step further, he could even target to the specific regions that he found better for testing and the most ideal marketing quarter of the year in which he would run such a program. The same basic principles that apply when utilizing any print or broadcast media can be applied to the selection of events and sports sponsorship properties.

Sponsorship is a Tough Sell

As many of us are aware, sponsorship is a tough sell when you are dealing in opportunities that sometimes look like operating budgets of small countries. There will always be the big boys who seem to have limitless desires to sponsor, of course, but the real winners in the event and property sponsorship game are the sellers who do their homework and tailor their presentations to potential sponsors with the sponsors best interest at heart. Don't get caught in the trap of trying to sell the big hit. It is difficult enough to get a sponsor to listen to what you have to say, so make sure that you say something that they want to hear. By doing that it shows that you really want the program to benefit the company, not just put a big commission in your pocket. If you play the sponsorship game this way, you will get more people to listen and buy. After all, a sponsor that has a good experience is going to continue to accept your phone calls. And the truth is, the one who doesn't have a good experience will forget your name.

Long-standing traditions in sponsorship are giving way to a more cost conscious future. Instead of spending millions of dollars to sponsor a single event, such as a tennis tournament, networking a variety of events together is the current wave. This allows companies flexibility and the best possible utilization of their monies.

116

Consumer Dialogue Is A Part of Sponsorship

Anything that can be done face-to-face with consumers can be done at special events as part of a sponsorship package. This is not a throw-in compensation but the basis for the decision to move forward, so don't trivialize the opportunity to point this out to the potential sponsor. Simmons Research has shown that attendees of special events, fairs in particular, have extremely high buying indexes. Recognize this and use this knowledge to analyze and design sponsorship offerings for your potential sponsors company's that meet their marketing strategies and goals.

A sponsorship should be viewed as a partnership with each entity bringing something to the table. Sponsorship can be an ideal way for companies to sample, test market, data capture, survey customers, distribute coupons, or simply enhance customer awareness. Knowing this to be the case, incorporating any or all of these benefits as part of the overall sponsor program is a must for you to achieve maximum results from your presentations. And, achieving this with an eye on the sponsor's expenditures and budget will make your presentation a most refreshing change of pace. Never forget that the sponsor that spends a few thousand dollars per event this year could potentially spend a few hundred thousand next year.

Chapter 50 – STRATEGIC SELLING: HOW TO BE MORE EFFECTIVE

Whether your event needs $5,000 or $5,000,000 in sponsorships, you need to have sales training and experience. However, many event people have never had formal training or experience selling anything. As a result, they make mistakes that alienate potential sponsors and, ultimately, lose sales.

The protocol of selling is actually very easy to learn. By following a formula of ten steps, you can increase your effectiveness as a salesperson and land more sponsorships than you ever thought possible.

Step 1. **Be goal-oriented**. In sales, as in any aspect of business, it is critical to be goal-oriented. If you don't have specific goals, you will not be able to measure your progress effectively and examine what you need to do to become better at your job. In order to set realistic goals, look at your sponsorship sales over the past two years. Has there been a steady rate of growth? Do you anticipate any activity that will impact your sales positively or negatively over the next year? Determine what level you need to reach in order to have a financially solvent event. Remember that your goals have to be reasonable. Unless there are extremely extenuating circumstances, you cannot expect to increase your sponsorship sales by 200 percent in one year. A more realistic goal would be 20-30 percent.

Step 2. **Write your goals down**. After you have taken the time and effort to set your goals, write them down. If you think you can skip that step, you are wrong. Goals that are not written down are just dreams. Turn your dreams into reality by picking up your pen. When not written down, goals become cloudy and may hinder the success of your plan. Writing your goals down is a great way to refresh your memory and keep you focused.

Step 3. **Know your product.** It is amazing how many people walk into a prospect's office without a thorough knowledge of the products or services they provide. Without such knowledge, there is no way to identify how you can fill the client's needs. Do your homework before you meet with a potential client. Know what you can -- and cannot -- provide, including various sponsorship benefits and rights. This way, you have all of the information you need to make an effective presentation and your sponsor will appreciate your respect for his or her time.

Step 4. **Identify the client's needs**. Selling a prospect a sponsorship that will not meet the client's objectives hampers your ability to build the long-term relationship you need to be a successful salesperson. The most effective salespeople see themselves as problem-solvers, identifying the barriers that their customers are facing and providing the tools to break down those barriers. Put yourself in your sponsor's shoes and try to determine how you can best help your sponsor accomplish his/her goals. Present your sponsorship with a benefits orientation. Make sure the prospect understands the benefits. Once understood, the prospect becomes a sponsor.

118

Step 5. **Never, never lie**. While pointing out benefits and offering additional benefits is important, it is even more important not to mislead the client in your presentation. Promising more than you can deliver is the quickest way to lose credibility and sponsors. If the prospect asks you something about which you are unsure, tell the prospect, "That's a good question. Let me get back to you on that." If the prospect asks you for something you know you cannot deliver, be honest and say so. Then, see if you can help the prospect resolve the situation in another way.

Step 6. **Pay attention to the details**. From maintaining a neat appearance to checking proposals for typographical errors, it is important to pay attention to the impression you are making. Once you make the sale, be sure that the product gets delivered and the sponsor gets regular updates. Attention to detail builds strong relationships and repeat sales.

Step 7. **Follow through**. At each point in the sales process, it is important to follow through to the next level. From calling on a hot lead to making sure that your proposal was received, not following through in sales is the equivalent of dropping the ball in a football game. Failure to follow through shows a lack of commitment and makes a bad impression on would-be clients.

Step 8. **Be tenacious**. Anyone who has been in sales for any length of time knows that getting a "yes" to a sales pitch on the first visit or through the first contact is a rare occurrence. Often, it takes a sales representative several contacts and repeated follow-through to prove him- or herself to a client. Estimates are that 90 percent of salespeople give up too soon. Perhaps the sponsorship is perfect for the client, but you have approached him or her at the wrong time. By being tenacious, continuing to provide the client with information and offering your services, you can ultimately reach the proper intersection of timing, need and action.

Step 9. **Know when to close and when to walk away**. You have followed all of the steps and have a prospect who seems very interested in sponsorship. Now is the time to ask for the order. There are many different ways to do this, and you will have to determine which is right for you. Unfortunately, in spite of your best efforts to be prepared, identify your client's needs, create a good impression and follow through diligently, there will be prospects who will not become sponsors. There comes a point in the sales process where, if the prospect becomes unreasonable or if you have come to an impasse, you need to walk away. Recognizing when you are wasting your time on a prospective sponsor with irrational demands or a budget that is too small is just as important as knowing when to close.

Step 10. **Get to work**. Once the sale is complete, you have only done 10 percent of the work. You must now ensure the best possible service. Keep in contact with your sponsors to stay on top of their progress. If there are any problems, handle them in a timely, professional manner. Make your sponsor feel as if he or she is your top priority. Follow through with all promised benefits and you can be assured of a renewal after your event.

The Harvard Business School did a study to determine the common characteristics of top salespeople. The evidence they found is clear that most people can be top sellers if they are willing to study, concentrate and focus on their performance. Here are the attributes the study found in highly successful salespeople:

- Did not take "no" personally and allow it to make them feel like a failure. They have high enough levels of confidence or self-esteem so that, although they may be disappointed, they are not devastated;

- 100% acceptance of responsibility for results. They didn't blame the economy, the competition, or their company for dips in closings. Instead, the worse things were, the harder they worked to make negatives work to their advantage;

- Above average ambition and desire to succeed. This is a key area because it affected priorities and how they spent their time on and off the job, with whom they associated, etc.

- High levels of empathy. The ability to put themselves in the customer's shoes, imagine needs and concerns and respond appropriately;

- Intensely goal-oriented. Always knowing what they were going after and how much progress they were making kept distractions from side-tracking them;

- Above-average will power and determination. No matter how tempted they were to give up, they persisted toward goals. Self-discipline was a key;

- Impeccably hones with self and the customer. No matter what the temptation to fudge, these people resisted and gained ongoing trust of customers;

- Ability to approach strangers even when it is uncomfortable.

How many did you rate high in? What should you be doing to help yourself? Selling is a great field filled with opportunity. But that opportunity must be utilized ... and that takes concentration and focus. The S-Myth™ (that's sales myth) --- salespeople are born, not made ... debunked again!

CHAPTER 51 – TIPS FOR SUCCESSFUL SPONSORSHIP SALES

Selling sponsorships is just like selling anything else; if you follow the principles of good salesmanship you will have greater success than your competitors. Each year we see an increase in lifestyle activities to sponsor. Dollar amounts invested in sponsorships continue to grow as more and more companies are recognizing the value of lifestyle marketing in helping them achieve their marketing objectives. All of this means there is more competition for corporate dollars.

How do you differentiate yourself from the competition? Here are 10 suggestions that will help increase your sponsorships sales and improve your renewals of existing sponsorships.

1. Produce quality materials.

How many times have you received a proposal with typos, misspelled names, page numbers out of sequence, poor quality photos, etc.? If you are trying to convince a prospective buyer of your professionalism, you must demonstrate it through your materials. Double check the spelling of the individual's name as well as his/her title, company name, and other pertinent information as it relates to each proposal. If you are customizing your presentation, make sure the company is referred to properly and make sure you have made a universal change throughout the presentation. And, don't just rely on the spelling checker in your computer -- read through your presentation before it goes out to the potential sponsor to ensure there are no errors.

2. Understand the sponsor's corporate culture.

Learn something about each company you are soliciting for sponsorship. If it is a publicly traded company, request a copy of the most recent annual report. Do a data search at the library, check industry periodicals for the last year, to get a sense of the company's media exposure and activities. Read trade newsletters so you have a clear picture of what the company is interested in and what their sponsorship expectations are. Understanding your customer is one of the first rules of successful consultative selling.

3. Understand your property.

As simplistic as this sounds, you must know your product. Know and understand all the opportunities that can be afforded your sponsor - hospitality, signage, tickets, product sampling, etc. Be prepared to provide your potential sponsors with photos, videos and other visual elements that will further enhance your sponsorship proposal and entire participation.

4. Have good follow-through.

Be consistent in your approach, deliver what you say you will, and be sensitive to the individual sponsor needs.

5. Demonstrate good selling skills.

One of the first skills is good listening. Your potential sponsors will quickly tell you what their marketing objectives are and how your program will, or won't, fit into their marketing program. If you agree it's not a good fit, move on to the next one. Don't waste time arguing or attempting to fit a square peg into a round hole. Conversely you may need to reposition your proposal to better comply with the potential sponsor's needs before giving up completely.

6. Maintain your sense of humor.

Selling sponsorships is serious! However, you can often get through a difficult negotiation process if you maintain your sense of humor. Keep in mind that difficult and/or tense negotiations can be eased with tasteful humor.

7. Be specific in your contract benefits.

When preparing the sponsorship contract, be specific in your listing of benefits and rights. For example, rather than say, "Sponsor has the right to hang four banners in highly visible locations," state "Sponsor has the right to hang four banners (size) at the following locations: _____." If all benefits and rights are clearly delineated, there is no room for misunderstanding.

8. Delineate responsibilities.

Within this same contract, define who is responsible for what. For example, in the previous instance, who will hang the banners and who will be responsible for taking them down, storing them, etc.? Again, spell out these responsibilities precisely so they are easily understood.

9. Deal with problems before they get out of hand.

No situation is perfect and no matter how clearly the contract is written, there are bound to be minor misunderstandings. Address them quickly, get clarification on matters where either side is confused, and get concurrence on the resolution of the problem(s). If handled quickly, problems can be eliminated and not allowed to compound and escalate.

10. Be honest.

Tell the truth about attendance, media exposure, former sponsor relationships. Don't lie because that won't lead to a long-term, trusting relationship. Honesty has long-term paybacks.

These ten tips will help you improve your sponsorship sales ratio as well as enhancing your renewals. And, remember, sponsorship sales are fun ... enjoy yourself!

Chapter 52 – RULES FOR SUCCESS

1. **Believe that you have already succeeded** before you even begin the task. Act, dress and speak not for who you are now but for who you want to be.

2. **Replace negative statements** with positive phrases. Tell yourself "I am a good person." "I am a success." Practice this before going to bed and upon waking in the morning.

3. **Take responsibility for your actions** and your life. Never allow yourself to blame others for your lack of success. Even though an event might be caused by someone else and is out of your control, control your own reaction to the event.

4. **Think positively** about all of your accomplishments, no matter how small they may appear to others. They are your building blocks of success.

5. **Formulate a mission statement** and keep it with you at all times.

6. **Remind yourself of great success stories** and the difficulties those people had in accomplishing their goals. Such examples as Helen Keller and Winston Churchill remind us that our problems and tribulations are small fish in a great sea.

7. **When taking on a new project** ask yourself: "What is the worst that can happen?"

8. **Allow yourself to make mistakes**. It is an essential growth component.

9. **Strive to be the best you can**, not the best there is. You may find, however, that one leads to the other.

10. **No one was born a great doctor, lawyer or salesperson**. We all came into the world as babies. We all become what we are based on the choices we make. You can choose success.

Chapter 53 – CHARACTERISTICS OF GOOD SALESPEOPLE

The two basic qualities that good salespeople must have are empathy and ego drive.

Ability to feel

Empathy, the important central ability to *feel* as the other person does, in order to be able to sell them a product or service, must be possessed in large measure. Having empathy does not necessarily mean being sympathetic. One can know what the other fellow feels without agreeing with that feeling. But salespeople simply cannot sell well without the invaluable and irreplaceable ability to get powerful feedback from the potential sponsor through empathy.

Need to conquer

The second of the basic qualities absolutely needed by good salespeople is a particular kind of ego drive which makes them want and need to make the sale in a personal or ego way, not merely for the money to be gained. The feeling must be that the sale must be made; the customers are there to help salespeople fulfill their personal need. In effect, to top salespeople, the sale -- the conquest -- provides a power means of enhancing the ego. Their self-picture improves dramatically by virtue of conquest, and diminishes with failure.

Because of the nature of all selling, salespeople will fail to sell more often than they will succeed. Thus, since failure tends to diminish their self-picture, their ego cannot be so weak that the poor self-picture continues for too long a time. Rather, the failure must act as a trigger-- as a motivation toward greater efforts – which, with success, will bring the ego enhancements needed. A subtle balance must be found between (a) an ego partially weakened in precisely the right way to need a great deal of enhancement (the sale) and (b) an ego sufficiently strong to be motivated by failure but not shattered by it.

The salesperson's empathy, coupled with his/her intense ego drive, enables him/her to hone in on the target effectively and make the sale. Salespeople have the drive - the need to make the sale - and empathy gives them the connecting tool with which to do it.

Synergistic effects

People with a strong ego drive have maximum motivation to fully capitalize on whatever empathy they possess. Needing the sale, they are not likely to let their empathy spill over and become sympathy. Their ego need for the conquest is not likely to allow them to side with the customer; rather, it spurs them on to use their knowledge of the customer fully to make the sale.

On the other hand, salespeople with little or no ego drive are hardly likely to use their empathy in a persuasive manner. They understand people and may know perfectly well what things to say to close the sale effectively, but their understanding is apt to

124

become sympathy. It they do not need the conquest, their very knowledge of the real needs of the potential customer may tell them that the customer, in fact, should not buy. Since they do not need the sale in an *inner* personal sense, they may not persuade the customer to buy.

Thus, there is a dynamic relationship between empathy and ego drive. It takes a combination of the two, each working to reinforce the other -- each enabling the other to be fully utilized -- to make the successful salesperson. Keeping these two aspects in balance -- empathy and ego drive -- will help you be more successful in your sponsorship solicitations.

Once you have an understanding of empathy and ego drive your next step is to understand the psychology of selling. But, first, ask yourself the following six questions:

1. Am I proud to be a salesperson?

2. Am I in the top 20% of salespeople?

3. Do I genuinely like myself?

4. Is there any aspect of selling that makes me uncomfortable?

5. Does my self-concept include a high level of income?

6. Can I cope with the rejection that I will inevitably encounter in selling?

The most important thing you have to understand in the world of selling is that nothing happens until the sale takes place. And, in selling, the 80-20 rule, or the Pareto principle, prevails. According to the 80-20 rule, 80% of sales are made by 20% of the salespeople. And, once you get into the top 20%, you don't have to worry about money or employment again.

Selling is an inner game. That is, what is going on inside the mind of the salesperson makes all the difference to his/her success. We know there is a direct relationship between a salesperson's self-concept and his/her sales performance and effectiveness. You will feel uncomfortable if you don't act in accordance with your self-concept. And, you will always sell in a manner consistent with your self-concept. Some of us are uneasy about picking up the telephone and calling somebody. Others of us are uncomfortable about closing. By becoming more skilled, we feel more competent, raise our self-concept, and become more successful.

The core of self-concept is self-esteem. People with high self-esteem like themselves. How much you like yourself is the key determinant of your performance and your effectiveness in everything you do.

There are two major obstacles in selling. The first obstacle is the customer's fear of making a mistake. The second major obstacle in selling is the salesperson's fear of rejection. Until salespeople develop confidence, a high self-concept and sufficient resilience to bounce back from inevitable rejection, they cannot sell successfully. All outstanding salespeople have reached the point where they no longer fear rejection.

Sales are usually based on friendship. People will not buy from you until they are genuinely convinced that you are their friend and are acting in their best interest. There is a direct relationship between your level of self-esteem and how well you get along with different people. The best salespeople have a natural ability to make friends easily with prospective customers.

A key element in selling is enthusiasm and a passion for what you are doing. A sale is a transfer of your enthusiasm and passion about your sponsorship opportunity into the mind and heart of the other person.

The reason so may people fail in sales is that they do not stay with it long enough to get those first few winning experiences that raise their self-esteem and self-concept and set them off on a successful career in selling. That's why it's so important that, from the very beginning, you say to yourself that nothing is going to stop you until you are successful!

Shared qualities of top sellers

The Harvard Business School did a study to determine the common characteristics of top salespeople. The evidence they found is clear that most people can be top sellers if they are willing to study, concentrate and focus on their performance. Here are the attributes the study found in highly successful salespeople:

- Did not take "no" personally and allow it to make them feel like a failure. They have high enough levels of confidence or self-esteem so that, although they may be disappointed, they are not devastated;

- 100% acceptance of responsibility for results. They didn't blame the economy, the competition, or their company for dips in closings. Instead, the worse things were, the harder they worked to make negatives work to their advantage;

- Above average ambition and desire to succeed. This is a key area because it affected priorities and how they spent their time on and off the job, with whom they associated, etc.

- High levels of empathy. The ability to put themselves in the customer's shoes, imagine needs and concerns and respond appropriately;

- Intensely goal-oriented. Always knowing what they were going after and how much progress they were making kept distractions from side-tracking them;

- Above-average will power and determination. No matter how tempted they were to give up, they persisted toward goals. Self-discipline was a key;

- Impeccably hones with self and the customer. No matter what the temptation to fudge, these people resisted and gained ongoing trust of customers;

- Ability to approach strangers even when it is uncomfortable.

How many did you rate high in? What should you be doing to help yourself?
Selling is a great field filled with opportunity. But that opportunity must be utilized ...
and that takes concentration and focus. The S-Myth™ (that's sales myth) ---
salespeople are born, not made ... debunked again!

Chapter 54 – TWELVE REASONS WHY SALES-PEOPLE DON'T SUCCEED

1. **Not making enough calls.** You can't close people you don't call on. Remember, your competition is happy to make the extra effort.

2. **Not following through with promises made.** Prospects judge you by what you do, not by what you say. Be conservative with your promises and liberal with delivering on your promises.

3. **Not listening.** Your understanding of your prospect's unique needs will not increase by talking. Listen twice as hard and talk half as much and you'll double your sales.

4. **Not starting every day with a plan.** Set goals for each day and each week. Neil Armstrong did not land on the moon by accident. If you fail to plan, you plan to fail.

5. **Not describing customer benefits clearly, succinctly and persuasively.** Prospects are persuaded by "meaty" words, not "watery" sentences. Good presentations are short and the result of long preparation. What makes a poor presentation? Zero time spent on preparation!

6. **Not asking for the order often enough.** Failing to ask for the order is the same as asking for failure. Few customers buy on the first closing attempt. Successful salespeople ask for the order several times on each call.

7. **Negatively prejudging the prospects ability to buy.** If you imagine that your prospect won't buy, you're developing a self-fulfilling prophecy. Ask questions and check the facts but never discount the sale!

8. **Not dealing with customer objections head on.** When a prospect has an objection, welcome it as a question that you're happy to answer. Objections are often buying signals in disguise.

9. **Ignoring the power of a positive attitude.** When things don't go your way, change your attitude. A positive attitude will help you cope with failure, rejection and disappointment.

10. **Not changing and growing.** Welcome change as your friend. Granted, change and growth bring pain, but resisting change and growth lead to more failure and greater pain.

11. **Lack of focus on priorities.** Salespeople with a clear focus on the most important and most urgent tasks will always get better results than salespeople who allow themselves to get side-tracked.

12. **Failure to work harder and smarter.** Global competition will be won by people who are willing to work harder and smarter. Salespeople who quit early will be asked to leave sooner.

Common enemies of salespeople

The better we are at defeating the common enemies that all salespeople face, the more successful we will be. These enemies are:

Ego

Our egos make us think that what we have to say is more important than what the customer has to say, so we memorize product knowledge and dump data on any prospect who will stand still long enough to listen.

Too much talk

Because what we have to say is all-important, we pitch customers. The best salespeople know that the payoff in selling is far greater by asking the right questions, than for knowing the right answers. I have yet to hear of a salesperson listening himself out of a deal.

Poor listening habits

Because we talk too much, we listen poorly. If you truly want to listen better, don't talk. Nature abhors a vacuum and someone's words will rush in to fill the void. If they are not yours, they will be those of the customer. The person who talks will monopolize the conversation, while the person who listens will control the conversation.

Assumptions about what's on the customer's mind

Because we have been listening poorly, we think we know what the customer should want, rather than what she does want.

Talking about things that don't interest the customer

A carefully constructed, canned pitch will normally contain something like 20 feature benefits and the salesperson will tell the customer all about every one of them. This dumps the whole load on the customer, but customers buy for their reasons, not ours. Customers will usually have only one or two primary buying motives. Talking about other things only distracts, confuses and bores the customer.

Failing to determine the customer's attitude

A customer can have only one of three attitudes at any given time: acceptance, objection or indifference. If we know how to determine the customer's attitude accurately, and how to respond appropriately, we will be well on the way to a sale.

Not asking for the order

Our fragile egos tell us that if the customer rejects the offer, it is really a personal rejection. We feel slighted and fail to ask for a commitment of any kind. If you ask, you get. The more you ask, the more you get. If you don't ask, you don't get. It's just that simple.

Lack of well-defined goals and objectives

If you don't know where you're going, how will you know when you've arrived?

Not taking notes

If we don't write down what is important to the customer, we will forget and talk about what we think is important. The strongest memory is weaker than the palest ink.

Chapter 55 – THE PROCESS OF NEGOTIATIONS

PART 1 - LET'S MAKE A DEAL

What do the expressions "power breakfast", "the bargaining table", and "closing the deal" have in common? Each of these expressions conjures up visions of hard-core, winner-take-all negotiations. As event planners/managers, you participate in some form of negotiation each and every day. Whether it is finalizing a sponsorship proposal, securing staff for your event or meeting your fellow associates at the lunch table, it is safe to say the negotiation process consumes a large part of the day.

While each of us may know the process, few, if any, of us ever realize or, for that matter, ever appreciate the art/skill of negotiating - let alone do we recognize the steps involved in the process. Like anything, in order to master it, you must understand it. .

At the outset of our discussion, it is important to note that the negotiating process has little to do with traditional legal doctrines, except perhaps those of basic contract law. Instead, the negotiating process is governed by the same psychological, sociological and communicational principles which influence other interpersonal relations in our lives. The most important skill of a negotiator is that ability to recognize and cater to the personal needs of your adversary. Such basic skills usually impact the process more than your actual knowledge and understanding of the subject matter. Sometimes, interpersonal skills may even help hide your ignorance on the subject matter.

As such, the first, and to some extent the most important, concept to understand is when does the negotiation process actually begin? Does it begin at the bargaining table, the conference room or somewhere else? Take the following description of the commencement of a negotiation as an example:

> "Our opponents suggested that we meet on Wednesday evening at 8:00 and we agreed. They then proposed that we get together at their offices and we concurred. After we arrived at 8:00, they generously provided us with refreshments. We discussed the basketball game that had taken place the night before. After approximately thirty minutes of such conversation, the negotiations began."

Question: What is wrong with this description? If it is not obvious to you - pay attention. Consider that in this brief description, one party conceded the day, the time and the location for the negotiations and then permitted their opponents to create a feeling of obligation which might, in some way, influence the outcome through the offer of food and drink - all before the one party even realized that the negotiation process had already begun. While it is arguable whether or not such concessions may affect the outcome of negotiations, it is important to understand that they could. Remember, personal interaction has a way of influencing every phase of our life, so why not the negotiation process as well. The next time you hear small talk at the

131

bargaining table, realize it means something, something that is a part of the process (i.e., developing a relationship which will help influence the process, a stall tactic, etc.).

The first lesson of negotiations is therefore to know when and where the process begins. Negotiating is a process - a process with a start, middle and finish - all of which take time to develop. As with all things, certain identifiable stages have to occur in every negotiation. Stage 1 is when the negotiation process begins. As you can see from the previous example, negotiations began well before the actual meeting and prior to the first handshake. The process begins at the time of first contact, whether it is in person or by phone. Believe it or not, the point of first introduction, as in any relationship, sets the tone, defines the roles of the parties (i.e., dominant/submissive, aggressor/pacifist, open/subtle) and creates a personal tie between the adversaries. Whether or not you agree, it is a fact that the first interaction between the parties begins the negotiation process. So, next time pay attention to first introductions and be the one that influences the outcome with your interpersonal skills. In other words, charm them!!!

Part 2 - Non-Verbal Communications

The ability to communicate is what next defines the relationship between the parties and, in large part, establishes the atmosphere in which negotiations will proceed. From the moment discussions begin, your skill to communicate will be challenged. Ultimately your response to that challenge will be a critical factor in determining the outcome of your negotiations.

The ability to communicate is typically broken down into two forms -- verbal and non-verbal. While we all are capable of verbal communication, how many recognize -- let alone pay attention to and understand -- non-verbal forms of communication. Both forms are equally important to the negotiation process. Non-verbal forms of communication are, however, typically overlooked.

Indeed, one of the most important sources of information available to negotiators comes in the form of non-verbal communication. While parties generally concentrate on what is verbally communicated, most, if not all, fail to focus on the non-verbal signals emanating from the opposing party. In fact, some negotiators naively believe there is no need to look for such messages, since no competent negotiator would be so careless as to divulge important information in such an inadvertent manner. Well, guess again. Consider the fact that most theatrical performances by trained actors rarely eliminate all involuntary gestures or mannerisms of their own when they are "in character". If professionals are unable to avoid such unintended disclosures, then surely most untrained negotiators will experience less success in this regard.

Unless you can train yourself to appreciate these subtle non-verbal signs, you will never be able to fully understand and manipulate the negotiation process you are involved in to your advantage. The most obvious forms of non-verbal communication are facial expression and hand gestures. Following is a highlight of some of these gestures and what significance they may be interpreted to have.

- **Sitting on the edge of one's chair:** Typically such action indicates increased interest on the part of your adversary. If such action is correct, it suggests that your opponent is approaching an area or level he/she will be agreeable with. Push to close the deal.

- **Wringing hands:** Such action reveals tension or frustration, relaying a message to you that this topic is one of sensitivity and should be addressed delicately or at a later time when more of the negotiation process has been developed.

- **Hands folded on lap:** A position of this nature usually represents submissiveness. If it seems to fit the profile of your opponent, you should encourage this attitude and take advantage of it. In such an atmosphere, your opponent may feel more comfortable and, as a result, more agreeable.

- **Leaning back in chair/hands on back of head:** This reclining action is a sign of confidence and may be perceived as a mark of dominance. It is usually a reflection of the fact that your opponent believes things are going his way. Take note and proceed cautiously.

- **Palm of hand over heart:** This is an opponent's attempt to be sincere or credible. In such instance, this gesture must be weighed against the situation at hand and the other simultaneous communications of your adversary to determine if it is genuine. If it is, your opponent may be indicating that this is the best he has to offer. At this point, it may therefore be wise not to push any harder on that point of negotiation.

- **Open or uplifted hands:** This posture is normally expected when one is being given a true final offer -- it reflects an air of openness and sincerity.

- **Fingers of hands in a church steeple image:** Such an action again reflects confidence. Negotiators who notice such positioning should be careful they are not giving away more than is necessary.

- **Crossed arms:** This mannerism reflects a defensive, unreceptive posture, meaning it may be best to "back off" and approach that particular subject from another angle.

- **Crossed legs:** This stance constitutes a competitive or combative attitude. If such a posture occurs, it may be in the best interest of all parties to develop a better personal relationship before continuing negotiations. Charm them more before discussing the details of your negotiation.

- **Clenched teeth:** This facial expression reveals anxiety or anger. A good negotiator will work to ease this tension if the negotiation process is to continue.

- **Rubbing one's eyes:** Such a gesture means that your adversary is having a hard time accepting your concepts. Most times actions of this nature mean that your opponent is not readily accepting your explanation -- so keep discussing and educating your opponent until he/she understands. Otherwise, your position will never be factored into his/her negotiation strategy (i.e., there will be no concessions for your point of view).

133

- **Casual touching:** Such a gesture indicates an opponent's attempt at sincerity. At times, this action is also used to strengthen the interpersonal relation between the parties. Good or bad, it is a technique aimed at developing rapport. Unfortunately, it may also be used to brush over a weak spot in their negotiation. So, pay attention and do not be lulled asleep.

- **Direct eye contact:** As is often stated, this common expression is aimed at showing the truth of the matter. Most negotiators who can maintain such eye contact usually develop enhanced credibility and truthfulness.

- **Head nodding:** While most think this action represents agreeableness, it also may be used to keep the conversation moving. Obviously, it is important to know the difference. Pay attention to the totality of the circumstances to assess your opponent's real meaning.

If nothing else, looking for these gestures may help you locate "double messages" (i.e., an adversary verbally states one position while non-verbally relaying another) and force you to reassess/re-explore that part of the negotiation process before moving on to other topics. In other words, it may "red flag" the trouble areas of your position and help you create a "gut" instinct on the matter at hand.

Pay attention to the entire communication process. By noticing the non-verbal gestures in relation to their verbal response, a sense will develop within you as to the genuineness of the representations being made by your opponent. As such a sense is developed, it will therefore be easier for you to know when a fair deal has been struck in your favor.

Part 3 - Be Prepared

There is one rule for successful negotiating - like the Boy Scouts say - "Be prepared".

In the world of negotiations, preparation means research, research, and more research. In the world of event planning and sponsorship sales, preparation means knowing your trade and researching your industry standards. First, mission statements, corporate portfolios, and any other available background material on your negotiating counterpart must be read (i.e. needs and goals, budget concerns, industry position, company standards). Second, research must be done on how others in your business have presented, posed or "pitched" the concept you wish to negotiate. Remember, rarely are there many new ideas in this industry. Success, instead, hinges upon the presentation and/or style in which you introduce an idea. Why not know what has worked in the past. Information in this arena may be a little harder to come by. I suggest discussions with colleagues and the reading of various trade magazines to monitor your negotiating counterpart's activity in the event and sponsorship industry.

Research, unfortunately, does not stop there. There is one more level to investigate – know your individual counterpart at the negotiating table. Find out what makes your opponent tick. In the legal world that means read case decisions and opinions written by the Judge and other attorneys involved in the matter. In event planning/sponsorship sales that means talk to your colleagues and so-called "experts" in the field about your counterpart. Know what they have to say about your counterpart's reputation for fair dealing, his/her authority to close a deal, his/her honesty and trustworthiness, and his/her personal likes/dislikes. In other words, preparation means thoroughly researching all levels of the negotiating process from the players involved to the subject matter at hand. How else will you know if a fair deal has been presented to you?

It is to your best advantage to have all available weapons (i.e. resources) at your disposal **before** you sit down at the negotiating table. To do otherwise is like fighting with one hand tied behind your back or going into a gun battle with only one bullet in your revolver. Common sense would prevent most of us from allowing those scenarios to occur. In a similar fashion, do not demean your event's goals or missions by ignoring the subject matter upon which you are negotiating. Security, food vendors, insurance and sponsorship sales are a wide variety of subjects to be conversant in. Each of these subjects, as well as many, many more is crucial to the success of your event. So, do not compromise that success by lack of preparation. Failure to prepare will not result in the outcome you want but will result in an outcome dictated and controlled by your counterpart, if there is any agreement at all.

When your research is done, create an outline of your negotiating points in order of priority. Next to each point write down what you wish to accomplish if all things go perfectly. Next to that entry write down what the accepted standard/practice is in the industry on that point or, if none exists, your own bottom line. Without much effort these resulting notes create a range of settlement - a range that provides you a zone of comfort in which to negotiate. Furthermore, the research outlined in front of you will provide the facts and figures to support your position - a position that, if researched well, will clearly indicate how far a particular point can be pushed. In short, the outline, or as some like to call it, the "wish list", will summarize your research and provide you with a clear cut negotiating range for each point of concern.

What does all this mean? Do your homework before negotiations begin. The fruits of your hard work will develop, direct and ultimately control the negotiating process.

Part 4 - Let the Negotiations Begin

After being primed on three basic concepts:

- Knowing when the negotiation process begins;
- Understanding your opponent's body language; and
- Being prepared on the subject matter,

... you are ready to actually negotiate. So, please grab a chair and sit down at the bargaining table.

At this point, your ability to use these three concepts (for better or for worse) will be challenged. It is not as simple as making an offer, arguing your point and making a deal; a lot more goes on. And, a good negotiator makes a point to understand how every step of the process works. In fact, while at the bargaining table, your ability will

135

be challenged over a series of distinct phases -- phases that occur routinely in each and every negotiation, whether we pay attention to it or not.

Phase 1: The Information Phase*

The first distinct phase of negotiations begins with the information phase. Upon conclusion of the introductory "chit chat", conversation usually changes to the specific details of the subject matter at hand. This change in the conversation introduces you to the start of the Information Phase.

The purpose of this phase is to explore and understand the needs, interests, and objectives of the opposing party. Typical questions* asked during this exploratory step are:

1. What is it that you need to obtain?

2. Why do you hope to achieve that?

3. What terms might alternatively satisfy the needs and interests of your client?

4. What do you think_____ might provide you with what you really have to have?

5. What will you do if this deal does **not** go through?

Similar to the first jab of a boxing match, this phase is a negotiator's way of feeling out an adversary. From outlining the critical issues to be discussed to secretly challenging an opponent's knowledge of the subject matter, a rough draft or script is developed for the ensuing negotiations. If nothing more, through the process, the parties will outline the issues (i.e. disputes) that divide them.

What is omitted from this phase is your bottom line position and what influences or controls your decisions.

Phase 2 - The Competitive/Distributive Phase*

Once the rough draft is in place, conversation begins to focus. Discussion changes from what you hope to achieve to what you must obtain to close the deal. This phase is defined as the Competitive/Distributive phase. It is at this point that "hard core" negotiations actually begin.

Typical issues* during this phase are:

1. If this meeting is going to be beneficial to both of us, I must obtain at least _____.

2. If I cannot get _____, this situation cannot be amicably resolved.

3. I am not in a position to offer you more than _____; and

4. As I understand it, I believe you are not entitled to more than _____.

As you can see, during this phase, the issues no longer concern the others' objectives but, rather, focus on your own feelings/position. Real offers and counter offers are made at this point. Wish list items are no longer discussed. Positions form;

issues are divided; lines are drawn in the sand. Hence, the idea behind the term "competitive/ distributive".

With positions set, it is time to bargain. Fairness and an idea of equity are put on hold. Nothing is truly fair at this juncture. Instead, what is best for your cause is what prevails. A negotiator must diligently seek to advance his or her own interests. So, how do you do this? The answer is quite simple -- a touch of charm and a dash of common sense helps your persuasive power but what really counts are a whole lot of facts to support your reasoning. The facts will ultimately win the battle. As an aside, it is also a good idea to know your alternatives because, if you cannot walk away from a deal, your negotiating position is greatly compromised.

If done properly, concessions begin to emerge and issues dwindle. A good negotiator (or salesperson) peels away an opponent's problem like an onion -- one layer at a time. When the competitive phase is complete, a mutually acceptable agreement remains. To most the deal is done, but one politically correct step still remains.

Phase 3: The Cooperative Phase*

Although the dollar amounts may have been finalized in the competitive phase, there always remain certain non-quantifiable intangibles to be discussed. In other words, certain tradeoffs – tradeoffs not important to you but important to your opponent – should be made. Whether it be to "save face" or to reinforce a fair deal, it is great to close a deal by helping each other out. However, in order to do this, both sides must be open with each other. By cooperating, the parties can fine tune their underlying deal and allow both sides to leave the bargaining table with a feeling of accomplishment. When this phase is done, the deal is complete.

This is the "close the deal fairly" portion of your negotiation. No matter how much support is available for your position, never abuse your power. Common sense should make you realize that your opponents may surface on other deals. Keeping them happy now may lead to more benefits down the road.

Conclusion

Most negotiators are so anxious to close a deal, they tend to hurry through the phases described above. Unfortunately, such a "rush to judgment" is frequently counterproductive. Each phase sets a pace, establishes an atmosphere and creates an air for settlement. To gloss over them or to ignore them usually creates an uncertainty in your opponent – and uncertainty usually kills a deal.

As such, it is in your best interest to be conscious of each development state of the negotiation process. Pay attention, focus on the issues and let the negotiation process take its course. The results will end up in your favor if you pay attention to what you are doing.

*Claver, Charles B. **Effective Legal Negotiation and Settlement**, The Michie Company©. 1986, pp. 55-111.

Six Negotiation Strategies

With the right strategies we can all shape successful deals whether we are buying, selling, solving customers' problems, managing conflict or just dealing with difficult people.

To reach your objectives and exert a positive influence over others, you'll need a game plan for reaching agreement. Here are some strategies to help you achieve your objectives and create win-win deals:

Strategy No. 1: Be prepared

The key to success in any negotiating situation is preparation. As the saying goes, "Knowledge is power." The more you know about the circumstances surrounding the situation, the more powerful you will feel and the more you will be able to direct the outcome.

First, define the needs of the other party. Ask yourself, "What do I know about them?" This is particularly important because many salespeople assume that the buyer has all the power. The salesperson often feels powerless to control the outcome. By establishing how much the buyer needs of what the salesperson has to offer, you shift the balance of power. The degree to which the feeling of power and control will be transferred to the salesperson depends, to a large extent, on knowledge.

It is a simple truth of negotiations that the control of the negotiation will lie with the party that is perceived to need the deal the least. So take as much time as circumstances permit to evaluate the situation. There is no substitute for knowledge.

Strategy No. 2: Negotiate with top level decision makers

While this may seem obvious, there is more to this strategy. Always establish the decision-making hierarchy ahead of time. If you don't know who the decision maker is, aim high. This strategy will achieve three very important objectives:

1. The higher you reach in the decision-making process, the better you can assess the needs of the other party. For example, if you target the president of a company to negotiate with and you get to deal with him or her, your power base will be stronger because the need to strive for an agreement has been demonstrated at the highest level within the organization.

2. By aiming high you are more likely to be dealing with someone who can discuss options beyond simply "yes" and "no"... someone who can shape up a deal and not just respond to the situation as it appears at face value. This is an important tactic because if you negotiate at a lower level where only "yes" or "no" decisions can be made, you run the risk that if the answer is not "yes" it will have to be "no" - not ideal circumstances for a win-win outcome.

3. By dealing with the highest level of decision maker you will avoid many of the common barriers to business decisions. Policy, budgets, systems and higher

138

authority are often used as excuses to defer decisions and sometimes as negotiating ploys to secure concessions. If your negotiating partner is the ultimate decision maker, chances are these barriers will not exist.

Strategy No. 3: Get the agenda

Never open a negotiation with a demand or an offer. Always make sure you ask questions at the outset of the negotiation - questions to clarify the facts, gather information and establish needs. This is what I call "getting the agenda". If you don't take this initial step in the negotiation you run the real risk of agreeing to a deal without ever knowing if it was the best deal, or a fair deal, for both parties. Never, ever, deal without an agenda.

Strategy No. 4: Trade concessions; don't give them

Whenever you are required to give a concession in order to clinch the deal, always create a "quid pro quo," something for something. Not only does this strategy establish the fairness of the deal, thereby creating a win-win outcome, it also helps you maintain professional integrity. People have very little respect for you if you simply crumble under pressure. Don't give away the store. Remember, if you just give, they will just take. Always seek a trade.

Strategy No. 5: Play it cool

Understand the other party's emotional commitment. However, make sure you always have control of your own emotions during a negotiation. Never lose your temper or show excitement unless you know the other party well enough to be sure that he or she will not manipulate your vulnerable emotional state. Always avoid emotional seepage. As they say in poker games, "Play your cards close to your chest."

Strategy No. 6: Walk away from bad deals

All good negotiators understand the importance of maintaining an objective perspective about the outcome of any deal. A good negotiator won't even sit down to negotiate unless he or she is already prepared to get up and walk away. Never fall in love with the idea of doing deals. If you do, you will lose sight of your real objectives and work to satisfy the false goal of a deal at any price.

This six-part strategy requires that you evaluate your options to a successfully negotiated agreement. You will enter the negotiation feeling more powerful and in control - and more likely to secure a fair and equitable deal.

Negotiation Tips To Close More Sales

1. Know your needs and wants.

What do you want from the negotiation and why do you want it? Brainstorm, make a list and prioritize it. You may not get everything you want so make sure that you know what's most important. What is at stake? What is your time frame? What are your emotional needs?

2. Know the other person's needs, wants and goals.

Ask questions of the person or other people so you can find out some of their needs and goals. Put yourself in the other people's shoes and think the negotiation through from their point of view. What's in it for them? What's their bottom line? How soon do they have to make a decision? Try to imagine what their first offer might be, or how they might react to yours. What do you think they'll object to, and what offer do you think they'll accept? How will it make them look if they accept your offer? How do they need to feel after the negotiation? Do they need to appear fair? Look good with the company?

3. Decide who should negotiate.

Just because you have an interest in a situation, you may not be the appropriate one to negotiate. Perhaps you need more expertise. Maybe you're too emotionally involved. Will you be outnumbered in the negotiation? If so, maybe you'd be more comfortable if you brought along a colleague.

4. Determine the best time and place.

Most standard books recommend negotiating on your turf, but that's not always best, particularly if you don't want to intimidate the other side. If that's the case, their turf or neutral turf might be the best choice. Don't feel you must accept the physical situation. For example, if you go to someone's office and he or she is sitting in a huge chair behind a huge desk, and you are expected to sit on a much lower seat, you may feel at a psychological disadvantage. Suggest moving to a conference table or coffee table if it's available.

5. Develop a step-by-step strategy.

Have a plan A and plans B, C and D. Your first strategy might not work with certain people. Negotiation can be very creative. Don't bank on your original idea being the one they'll respond to. Remain as flexible as you possibly can throughout the negotiation process. Be prepared to shift gears to counter any changes in approach by the other side.

Negotiating Successfully By Phone

Negotiating by phone is an essential sponsorship sales skill but one that is overlooked and underrated.

Try these tips to help you strike a deal or clinch a sale, while also creating a win-win situation for all parties involved.

The person who makes the phone call has the advantage.

You get a surprise call and suddenly you're on the speakerphone with your prospect and your prospect's colleagues -- all ready to pummel you with questions and concession requests. Ask if you can call them back so you can collect all of your information. That way, you'll have time to prepare details and strategy.

When you are the one making the call, make sure you find out if now is a good time to talk. You don't want to attempt to get their full attention if they are in a meeting or just heading out the door.

Get the other party to make the first offer.

The other party might be feeling generous -- or they may be in a more cautious mode. They might give you more than you anticipated, putting you in a great position. Even if the deal isn't quite right, at least you know where to start. And, when they make the first offer, it might be higher than what you had planned!

Avoid counterproposals.

Ask questions when someone presents you with an offer. Using this strategy, you can work on their proposal's shortcomings instead of offering one of your own.

Ask them to make easy decisions.

Boil down your offer to simple terms, especially if your sponsorship is complex. If you can get agreement one step at a time, it's much easier than asking your prospect to make a major yes/no decision on everything at once.

Don't show desperation.

Even if you have an event starting tomorrow and still don't have a major sponsor, don't let your desperation show. You'll put yourself in a weak negotiating position.

Trade your concessions.

This creates a win-win opportunity, so both parties get something in a deal. *"If I drop the price, which of the benefits do you feel we could leave out?"*

Show a little pain when making concessions.

Go ahead, whine and groan a bit. Don't start out with *"Here's the price, but I might be able to do better."* Otherwise, your prospect will be ready to sharpen the knife and slice the offering. Also, deliver the price in a confident, upbeat voice. Don't raise your voice like a question mark at the end; ending on that note surely leads the prospect to negotiate for a cheaper deal.

Before agreeing to a concession, get a commitment to buy.

Too many sales reps cave in to a price demand and then are blindsided with another concession. Ensure that this doesn't happen. *"If I can do this for you, I'm assuming we will go ahead with the sponsorship as planned, right?"* Be sure they know the concession is good only if they buy and that it's not a starting point for more negotiations.

Follow up in writing.

Recap your telephone conversation by sending a letter, fax, or e-mail. Do this quickly while the discussion is still fresh. It's an important gesture to cement the relationship with your prospect -- and it's a comfortable way to clarify anything that was vague.

Chapter 56 – FIVE MINUTES TO BETTER LISTENING

Improve your closing ratios by sharpening your listening skills.
Here are five easy, one-minute steps to help you achieve more sales.

1. Listen with all of your senses

Human beings have five senses: hearing, touch, smell, sight and taste. Focus each of your senses completely and totally on your prospect's words and underlying messages. During your presentations, avoid such distractions as doodling (touch and sight) or chewing gum (smell, taste and touch). Focus all of your senses on your prospect and you'll "hear" more messages to help you sell.

2. Take notes

To help you remember what went on during the sales call, take notes of personal data, important comments and areas for additional probing. Refer to your notes during the call and on future calls.

3. Encourage people to tell you their story

Most people would love to share their personal "success story" with you. Let them share their trials and tribulations as they admit you to their "inner circle" of trusted advisors.

4. Encourage talking with verbal feedback

Tell your prospects you're listening and you want them to continue. How? With such phrases as "good," and "I see," "uh-huh," and "go on." These phrases are verbal "prompts" or "cues." They are short messages indicating that you hear their words, understand their message and want them to keep going.

5. Ask questions

Questions tell your prospect that you are interested in her and what she wants and needs. Asking questions allows you to control the direction and momentum of the discussion. Answering your questions is how your prospects will reveal their most important needs - and how they want to be sold.

After you've reviewed these five listening improvement tips, make two copies. Place one copy in your tickler file for review in 30 days and assign the other to your 60-day file. By repetitive review and incorporation into your presentations, you'll improve your listening - and your sales.

Chapter 57 – IF YOU VISUALIZE IT, IT WILL HAPPEN

In one episode of the popular 1970's sitcom, The Brady Bunch, the oldest Brady girl, Marsha, successfully completes her driving test by imagining her proctor is wearing only undergarments.

While it's true that using one's imagination is the key to reaching goals, groovy Marsha might have been better off if she'd pictured herself successfully completing the test rather than focusing on someone else, say experts in the art of visualization.

Numerous studies have revealed that those who use visualization - the practice of creating positive mental images in one's mind - are much more likely to reach their goals than those who don't.

"If you can truly imagine yourself doing something, chances are you can do it," says Dr. Irene Bell, an Alexandria, Virginia based sports psychologist.

How does visualization work? Experts say that our brains are incapable of distinguishing between what is real and what is imagined; once you visualize something, you begin to believe that it will happen.

Although you might think you've never used any visualization techniques, chances are that you have - but probably in a negative way, according to Lisa Jamison, director at the Safety Harbor Resort and Spa in Safety Harbor, Florida. Most of us have pictured ourselves in a variety of nightmarish scenarios before, be it a meeting that takes a turn for the worst, or a boss taking us to task. "If you perceive negative, you will follow the negative path and get a negative response," Jamison says. The trick, she continues, is to turn our negative images into positive ones.

Below are some of Jamison's strategies for successful visualization:

- Practice visualizing and imagining with all your senses. Try to develop and sharpen your ability to create vivid mental pictures of people, places, and events through practice.

- The more vivid and detailed your mental images, the more powerful are the effects (for example, try to visualize in color).

- Before you physically or verbally practice a difficult task, mentally rehearse it. Your mental rehearsal will increase your overall preparation. For example, imagine yourself delivering a speech in a cool and confident manner before you practice in front of the bathroom mirror.

- When you are ready to physically practice the difficult task, photograph or videotape yourself completing it. Now you will have a tangible picture of yourself overcoming your anxiety to refer to if your confidence sags.

- Mentally rehearse helpful responses to difficult situations. Rather than getting discouraged, angry or anxious, see yourself staying confident, calm and positive.

- Work hard every day to change and reconstruct your negative, self-defeating self-images into positive, constructive ones.

- Establish a regular visualization practice routine. For the best results, visualization should be practiced when you are relaxed and quiet. Many short sessions (approximately five minutes each) are much better than one or two long sessions.

Jamison and other visualization gurus stress that visualizing something is not magic and doesn't replace physical practice; instead, it serves to put us in the right frame of mind to do what we need to do to succeed.

Chapter 58 – DEALING WITH VOICE MAIL
Here's how to get your prospects to return your call

There is no 100 % sure-fire way to reach people who insist on hiding, but here are a few things you can do to increase your chances.

- **Leave a message**

Some salespeople leave messages on the voice mail of prospects and some don't. Leaving a message can have an up side, but there are a few things to consider.

First, be ready to leave your message. Know exactly what you're going to say. Leaving a strong, articulate message will create a positive impression, and may get a return call (but don't count on it). A weak, bumbling message will create a negative impression and set you back a step. Keep the message upbeat and brief.

Second, leaving a strong message can help to "warm up" the prospect once you make a voice contact. The down side of leaving a message with a prospect (someone with whom you have little or no relationship) is that you now have to wait several days before calling back. You don't want to appear pushy, so you need to leave them time to return your call, even though you know the prospect is unlikely to call you.

Also you could say in your message that you will be calling back. That way it's OK for you to call back sooner.

- **Get to a human - fast!**

If your prospect's voice mail directs you to an assistant, talk to that assistant right away. If you're not sure there is an assistant, call the main number and ask. If there's no assistant, talk with the receptionist.

The first thing you want to find out from the assistant is if your prospect really is a prospect - is he or she the right contact for you. With that determined, you want to know if she usually picks up the phone when she is in, or are you likely to keep hitting her voice mail?

If your prospect usually picks up her phone when she's in the office, then you need to call a few times to reach her. If not, then your first job is to establish a relationship with this assistant (or receptionist) and your first sale is getting that person to help you reach your prospect.

- **Do's and don'ts**

  1. Don't open up with, "How are you today?" This screams "salesperson."

  2. Don't start out schmoozing or turning on the charm.

  3. Identify yourself in a professional manner. Give your name and company name. It's more professional and shows that you are not after anything except legitimate business.

4. Be prepared to discuss benefits in a genuine manner. Don't get into lengthy descriptions of your sponsorship. Get immediately to benefits and results. Keep it brief; don't waste time with your entire presentation.

5. Don't just send information on the request of the gatekeeper. Say that in order to send the right information you have to learn just a little about the organization and that a brief conversation with the boss will make that possible. If the screener insists that information be sent first, then ask permission to ask the screener a few questions. Make the screener feel important; someone whose opinion and observations you value. Sometimes you can get information that your prospect wouldn't reveal. I'll say something like this, "I'd be happy to send some information, but to make sure I send the right stuff, can I ask you a couple of quick questions?" No one has ever said "No.

6. Don't let an opportunity go by without learning something. If your prospect isn't in, but you reach a real person, ask questions.

7. Treat the gatekeeper with the same professionalism, honesty, good humor and sincerity you would your prospect.

8. Ask to make a telephone appointment with your prospect. If the gatekeeper likes you and sees a benefit in allowing you through, but you have trouble catching your prospect in, ask to make a telephone appointment. This has worked more than once. You may have several conversations with a gatekeeper before you are able to earn enough trust and become a business friend. It takes a little more time and persistence, but it's better than giving up.

- **Prospect knowledge**

You can increase the odds of getting a return call if your message demonstrates that you know a little about the prospect's organization.

If you leave a message like this: "Mr. Smith, this is Bill Cates with PowerPoint Printing, and I'm calling to introduce you to our company and explore how we might be able to serve your printing needs" you'll probably never hear from Mr. Smith again. But try this: "Mr. Smith, this is Bill Cates with PowerPoint Printing and I have a copy of your latest marketing packet here with me. It's a good-looking piece and I have a few ideas that I'd like to run by you that might help you further improve the effectiveness of this piece, without costing you any more." Now Mr. Smith knows you're thinking for him and that's valuable.

- **Calling when least expected**

Voice mail and gatekeepers are at maximum effectiveness during regular business hours. So try calling between 7:30 and 8:30 a.m., and after 5:00 p.m.

One word of caution when calling during fringe time. Your prospect may be working then to be free of all the normal interruptions of the day. Be very respectful of his time. If you can't make the appointment right away, go for a telephone appointment.

147

What could you send that would make your point, help you stand out from the crowd, and get your voice mail messages returned?

Regardless of what clever things you come up with, there is no substitute for getting to a real person and using your relationship skills to make a new business friend.

"Tag ... you're it" ... 8 Telephone Tag Tips

These easy steps will make your time on the telephone more productive:

1. Improve your timing.

Schedule your calls when you know your prospect will be in. Early morning, midweek, and midmonth are good times. Calls made on Monday mornings, Friday afternoons, and at the end of the month are likely to fail.

2. Have an alternative contact.

Develop a second or third contact within the company who can handle your calls if your first choice is unavailable.

3. Know thy gatekeepers.

The gatekeepers (secretary, receptionist, administrative assistant) often screen, field, and prioritize calls. Make friends with these people.

4. Know when to hold 'em; know when to fold 'em.

You waste precious minutes on hold that could be more productive. When your call is finally put through the target may be unprepared and not in the mood for another call.

5. Leave clever messages.

Define the desired action and time frame. Pique the target's interest or use a little light humor to get a smile and a return call -- but don't overdo it.

6. Make use of high-tech systems.

Don't let voice mail, answering machines, electronic mailboxes, or call processing put you off. These devices are for your convenience -- learn to use them to your advantage.

7. Get the important information.

Find out when the person will return, if he or she is expected to be busy then, and when the best time would be to attempt another call.

8. Know when to quit.

Stop calling when all methods have been exhausted.

Chapter 59 – HOW TO ADD VALUE TO EVERY SALES CALL ... Your skill is worth thousands

A salesperson's skill can add as much as 50 percent to the perceived value of any product or service. In many cases, particularly in service based industries, it can add much more. A high quality and professional approach is a powerful way to add value and differentiate yourself from your competitors.

Many top consulting firms carefully groom and train their senior consultants, knowing that how clients perceive them is as important as the work they carry out.

Ten Ways To Increase Your "Perceived Value" Rating:

1. Be well dressed

Most business people respect conservative attire more than fashion dressing. Make sure your clothes are well fitting and neatly pressed.

2. Invest in expensive or good quality accessories

These include your pen, watch, jewelry, briefcase, etc.

3. Have a tidy, neat, well-groomed appearance

Customers will appreciate your attention to details.

4. Practice impeccable manners, politeness and courtesy

Put your best self forward, all the time and to everyone.

5. Never knock the competition

If you do, you decrease your own value.

6. Be on time and deliver everything you promise

You are building your own reputation.

7. Never argue with customers

They may not always be right, but they are always the customers.

8. Look for opportunities to do something extra

Little things mean a lot. Send them articles on their company, call with information on their competition, etc.

9. Plan and prepare each appointment in advance

Don't leave things to chance or try to "wing it".

10. Write "Thank you" notes to each new customer or prospect

It doesn't cost anything to say thank you!

Bottom-Line Benefits

One of the surest ways to add real value in the mind of the customer is to focus your sales presentation around "bottom-line" benefits. Everybody, whether buying for personal or business reasons, can relate to these high value criteria:

- Saving money;

- Saving time (which is money);

- Improving satisfaction and quality levels;

Build a simple model into every sales presentation to help prospects cost-justify your sponsorship, showing specific, quantifiable savings in time or money over alternative solutions, as well as reinforcing the other benefits that comprise the entire offering.

Always make sure that your sales approach adds value by developing the most important bottom-line benefits - features your customers can measure in terms of improving quality above what they now have, or how your sponsorship can help save or make them time or money.

Chapter 60 – CLOSE THROUGH THE CUSTOMER'S EYES

At a banquet for real estate agents, the speaker introduced someone in the audience and said, "This man earned twice the national average in residential real estate sales last year."

The speaker's manner suggested that it was quite an achievement. But it wasn't all that impressive, so everyone craned his neck and looked at the man in puzzlement.

"...And he's totally blind." There was a burst of applause. When that quieted, the speaker said, "I'm sure that many of us are wondering how you got into the top third in sales achievement with that handicap."

"Wait a minute," the blind man replied over a portable microphone. "I don't have a handicap. I have an advantage over every other salesperson in this area. I've never seen a property I've sold, so I have to close my buyers through their eyes. What I'm forced to do, all you sighted people could do, and you'd serve your clients better and make more money if you did."

It was quiet in the hall for a moment while everyone thought that over, and then there was another spontaneous round of applause.

The point is, you must weigh the benefits and features and limitations of your product or service on your customer's scale of values, not your own; you must close on the benefits that are of value to him.

So, close your eyes and try to visualize and feel what your customer wants and needs. Listen to your customer's messages. Now sell to those needs and wants, not on the basis of what you want -or need- to sell.

Understanding Objections

When selling sponsorships you will often have to overcome objections. Objections are often comprised of two parts: the *stated* objection and the *real* objection.

Stated objections are usually the prospect's initial response when pressed for a decision or commitment and are sometimes referred to as "smoke screens". In many instances, these are emotional reactions to deep-seated concerns, such as fear of making a bad decision, loyalty to the competition, or a desire to withhold the real objection.

There is also the possibility that prospects aren't able to verbalize their concerns to you. When this occurs, you must help prospects both discover and verbalize their concerns.

Getting to the real objections

Unless you can get past stated objections by defusing the emotions involved, you won't get an opportunity to hear the real objections. Real objections represent the prospect's genuine concerns, doubts and questions. Resolving real objections is the key to helping the prospect make positive buying decision.

When a prospect voices an objection, respond by saying "You probably have a very good reason for saying that. May I ask what it is?" In this way you will get them past the initial objection. You may have to go through this three or four times before you either get rid of the objections or discover the real objection or cause for concern.

The three principles of answering objections

1. Don't argue.

Arguing establishes an adversarial relationship that destroys rather than builds trust;

2. Protect the prospect's ego.

Convincing prospects to agree with you often means they must admit to themselves and to you that their point of view was wrong. This is not easy for most people.

3. Lead prospects to answer their own objections.

Remember, if *you* say it, they may doubt it. But if **they** say it, it's true. Keep the prospect involved by using questioning and confirming statements that let the prospect get the answer to his or her own objection.

Conclusion

Objections offer you an additional opportunity for dialogue and negotiation. They tell you what concerns the prospective sponsor and, when verbalized, allow you to provide a reasonable explanation that eliminates that objection. Objections are just another way to get clarification.

Ten Steps To Closing Every Sale

Closing sales doesn't take magic. Just follow this simple 10-step plan:

1. Get your prospect to say "yes" right away.

As you talk to a customer, ask questions that he or she will answer "yes" to. This helps to establish the right frame of mind.

2. Keep digging for the reasons behind the prospect's objections.

Probe and question your prospect. To every objection, respond with: "You probably have a very good reason for saying that - may I ask what it is?"

3. Find out what the prospect wants.

Demonstrate how your sponsorship opportunity will help him/her get what he/she wants.

4. Sell benefits, not features.

This advice is familiar. Don't tell them they will get 100 tickets as part of your sponsorship; rather, you are providing them with employee, trade and client hospitality opportunities.

5. Concentrate on a single point.

Don't scatter your fire. Focus on a single point and don't get distracted.

6. Know when to shut up.

Many sales are lost because the salesperson kept talking past the point where the prospect was willing to buy. Learn how to read people and recognize when they're ready to buy.

7. Sell to the right person.

If you enlist the support of the people who'll actually be involved in the sponsorship, they'll help you persuade the person who makes the final decision on whether to buy.

8. Be persistent.

If a prospect is worth calling on, keep going back until you get the sale.

9. Clinch the sale.

Ask the prospect to sign the contract or letter of intent. This focuses the customer's mind on the signature, not on objections.

10. Reassure the prospect.

Stress that he/she has made a wise decision. Stress the benefits that will be enjoyed through the sponsorship. And, keep in touch during the entire program.

Chapter 61 – WHY A CONTRACT?

Before we even begin to answer that question, imagine the following scenarios: a dispute arises with a security company about personnel for the event; or the catering service fails to deliver the correct amount of food; or the wrong advertisement is printed in the local newspaper. Misunderstandings such as these, especially at the eleventh hour, can and do occur every day in an event manager's life.

As long as there are two parties to a business deal, there will always be two or more versions of that deal. Without some method of confirming, or at least supporting, your understanding, a business deal will always remain subject to interpretation. I'm sure most managers will agree, there is no room for surprises, eleventh-hour changes or misunderstandings in the life of an event.

Indeed, as the great New York Yankee, Yogi Berra, said, "I don't mind being surprised, as long as I know about it beforehand."

A written contract or agreement goes a long way toward minimizing or lessening the chance of last-minute surprises. If nothing else, a written contract will help point up potential problem areas in advance and give you the opportunity to prepare for them. It will not, however, guarantee that disputes or misunderstandings will not arise.

While no entirely satisfactory definition of the term "contract" has ever been devised, the most widely recognized legal definition is as follows:

"A contract is a promise or set of promises, for breach of which the law gives a remedy, or the performance of which the law in some way recognizes a duty."

It is no more than a set of instructions or directives created by the parties to explain each other's responsibilities and obligations; it is your own self-created private law of the transaction. The more simple and definite the terms of the agreement are, the more clear and concise the obligations of the parties to the "deal" are. Accuracy and clarity, therefore, underline the primary goal of any agreement; together, they produce clarity and avert misunderstanding.

Why a contract? Because the advantages of a written contract far outweigh any rationale behind a "handshake" deal or verbal agreement. An event manager's life has no room for surprises, and the most efficient method of minimizing and possibly eliminating them is by written contract.

154

Chapter 62 – UNDERSTANDING THE CONCEPTS OF CONTRACTS

What is a Contract?

A contract is an agreement to do, or not to do, a certain thing. In other words, a contract is a promise. If the promise is broken, the law provides a remedy. A contract may consist of a single promise or a series of promises that the parties regard as one contract.

What are the elements of a contract?

It is essential to the existence of a contract that there be:

1. Parties capable of contracting;

2. Mutual consent between the parties;

3. A lawful object to the contract; and

4. Sufficient cause or consideration for the contract.

1. Parties capable of contracting

All parties to a contract are considered legally competent except for:

    a. Minors (under the age of eighteen);

    b. People judged to be mentally insane or incompetent; and

    c. Those who are intoxicated by alcohol or drugs.

Each party to the contract must be legally competent in order for the contract to be valid. Each party to the contract must also have the authority of their corporate superiors to sign or execute the contract. If no such authority exists, no contract exists.

Therefore, an important first step in any contract negotiation is to determine that the party entering into the contract with you is legally competent and possesses the authority to sign such an agreement. Make sure you are involved with the "deal maker."

2. Mutual consent

Every contract requires mutual agreement or mutual consent. Usually, a party must intend to enter into a contract in order to be bound by it.

Mutual consent typically arises when one party makes an *offer* and the other party *accepts* it. The accepting party ***must accept the terms of the offer as it has been proposed***. If the accepting party attempts to vary an important term in the offer, the accepting party is only making a counter-offer. This is not a contract; the parties have not mutually agreed to its terms. If the counter-offer, however, is accepted "as is," then the parties have a contract.

155

In short, mutual assent is found when an offer is accepted unequivocally and unconditionally (i.e., without change). It is at this point and *only* this point that it can truly be said that the parties have met and a definite understanding between them has been created.

3. A lawful object

The object of a contract as well as the consideration in the contract must be lawful. Contracts to hire a "hitman" or to sell narcotics, for instance, are void and unenforceable in a court of law.

4. Sufficient cause or consideration

Consideration is often understood to be money, but no matter what, consideration must be something of value. Value can be an act, a forbearance, from acting or a promise. It may be a benefit agreed to be conferred on another or a detriment agreed to be suffered.

A contract, however, is only binding with consideration. Consideration is what distinguishes a contract from a gift, which may be unenforceable.

An agreement should always recite the consideration exchanged. This recital evidences the consideration. For example, agreements often state "for ten dollars and other valuable consideration..." Other agreements simply state the services to be rendered and the compensation for said services. These statements establish that there has been an exchange of value, even if it is nominal.

Finding these four elements in a written document, a letter, or in a purchase order means you have found the terms of a contract. Since event management professionals are drafting, negotiating, and signing contracts on a daily basis, I am certain you will find these elements appearing in almost everything you do. Contracts are used for everything from employing security personnel and making concession agreements, to renting facilities for the event. Without the presence of these elements, there is no contract. So before you "race off" to draft your first or your next contract, you should have a good general understanding of these principles. If not, some day, in some way, a mistake will occur and there will be no contract where one was thought to have existed. At that point, your problems will have just begun.

Chapter 63 – HOW TO DRAFT A CONTRACT

The easiest and most efficient way to begin drafting a contract is to start from scratch. The *first step* in drafting a contract is to take out a blank sheet of paper and set it down in front of you.

Too often, prepared forms or "fill-in-the-blank" agreements are where most event planners begin. This is unknowingly the first mistake event planners make. A form only tells you how another contract was drafted for a particular event, in a particular situation, at a particular time. Forms unfortunately never tell you how your specific event or your particular set of circumstances differ; and that is the main reason why forms inevitably lead to trouble.

Whether taken from a previous agreement or from a form book, a form is, at best, a guide. As a drafter, you must consider whether the language serves the purposes of the agreement you are drafting. To integrate form provisions into a working document, you must first understand the purpose served by each provision and how each provision interrelates with the others. If you don't understand this, how do you expect the document to be meaningful to your deal?

Remember, a contract is no more or less than a set of instructions or directives created by the parties to explain each other's responsibilities. The more simple and concise the terms, the easier it is to understand each other's responsibilities. Accuracy and clarity are, therefore, the underlying goal of any written agreement. Excess words or unnecessary provisions only "cloud" your agreement and create the opportunity for a misunderstanding. Understanding the language of your agreement is best ensured by starting from scratch.

Once the blank sheet of paper is before you, it is important to realize that the next step to drafting a contract is to ask questions -- lots and lots of questions! In fact, question everything -- who, what, why, where, when, how, and, of course, how much. After asking each question, respond to it in detail and with as much specificity as possible. These answers are the basis of your first draft of the contract.

For example, in a sponsorship contract, the following questions must be asked and answered.

Sponsorship Fee

- How paid?
- When paid?
- Refundable?
- Sponsor's right to renew? Right of first refusal?

Signs at Event

- How many?
- What is the size and placement of sponsor's name relative to others?
- Who pays for creating signs?

- Distance from other signs?
- Any conflicts with permanent signage at venue?

Advertising Credits

- On stationery?
- In name of event?
- On program cover?
- On souvenirs?
- In press releases?
- In print advertising?
- Can sponsor sell own souvenirs at event? (profit arrangement)

Public Relations/Personal Appearance

- Can promoter commit key event personnel or talent for sponsor appearance?
- Hospitality arrangements?
- Does sponsor get free tickets? How many?

Write down answers to each of your questions on the blank sheet of paper in front of you in as simple and concise sentences as possible. Speak English. (Note: the same type of detailed questioning can be done when drafting a security contract, a venue agreement or concessions deal. The idea is to brainstorm questions for every conceivable situation involved.) When all the questions are answered, reorganize the sentences in categories (i.e., fees, signage, etc.) Once this is done, the basic terms and parameters of your contract are before you; all that is left is to refine the language and, most important, provide for problems.

Much later, after this exercise is complete, look at the forms and use them as a guide to finalizing your contract. To do so any earlier only creates the chance of mistake, and mistakes are any event planner's worst nightmare.

STEP 1

It can be said that a contract can be broken down into the following bare essentials:

1. Basic terms;
2. Liability provisions; and
3. Standard boilerplate language.

The drafting of a contract is not a one step, form-oriented process. It is, instead, an interactive question and answer session, constantly testing whether the language of the contract is clear and determining whether there is a mutual understanding of the terms between the parties. As such, the next logical step to drafting a contract is to take those "basic terms" and formulate them into clear, definite and easily understandable sentences.

158

The best way to explain is to provide examples. The sentence structure of your draft contract should be similar to the following:

Exclusivity: The event hereby grants sponsor the right to be the "Official" sponsor of the event. The sponsor shall have the right to use the name of the event [and the trademark/logo (if applicable)] as well as the names and likenesses of the participants in advertising prior to and for (insert #) months after the event in connection with said sponsorship, provided the names of the participants are not used as an endorsement of any product or service. All such materials are subject to the event's prior written approval.

Signage: The event shall provide sponsor with (insert #) signs at the event. The creation and/or production of the signs shall be at the sponsor's sole expense. The signs shall be no larger than (insert dimension) and placed at the following event locations: (insert locations).

Advertising credits: Event shall give sponsor credit as a sponsor in all advertising and promotional materials prepared by event in the following form: "(insert form)".

P.A. Announcements: Event shall deliver (insert #) promotional announcements acceptable to sponsor over the p.a. system during the course of the event.

Obligations of the parties:

a. At the event's expense, event will organize, promote, produce, run and perform all acts necessary for the holding of the event.

b. For the rights granted to sponsor during the term of the agreement, sponsor shall pay event (insert $ amount), payable to event at the address designated above. (If paid in installments, add the following sentence) The payment of the contract fee shall be made in the following installments:

1. Amount, due date;

2. Amount, due date.

Simple sentence structure, like the above examples, makes the terms of an agreement definite. The more definitive the terms, the easier it is to understand each parties' responsibilities. And if the responsibilities of the parties are understood, it can be stated with confidence that a contract has been formed.

That brings us to the second essential element of a contract - the liability provisions, or those provisions that provide, in advance, for conflict resolution between the parties.

STEP 2

The second step to drafting a contract is to determine which terms of the draft may create conflict or create liability issues. In order to understand this second step, however, it is first necessary to understand "how an attorney thinks."

Notwithstanding the benefit of law school and the experience of private practice, the process of thinking like an attorney can actually be summarized in three easy-to-remember phrases:

Step 1: Predict - Predict what may happen;

Step 2: Provide - Provide for that event; and

Step 3: Protect - Protect yourself with a remedy.

The application of this three-step thought process to each of the basic terms and sentence structures of your draft will quickly highlight the problem areas or liability issues of your contract. For example, an event's use of a sponsor's logo/trademark may seem innocent at first glance. But to a sponsor, the use of its trademark/logo is one of, if not the most, valuable assets that it owns. Therefore, when reviewing the advertising credits (or any other term where a sponsor's trademark is used) in your contract, it is important to realize the sensitivity of this issue and the potential for dispute. A sponsor is very protective of its trademark/logo; therefore, some type of monitoring system must be created to reassure a sponsor that it will indeed be protected. Once recognized, such a dispute can be avoided by simply adding a "quality control" or "prior approval" paragraph. In other words, an event should provide the sponsor with the right to approve and authorize all advertising or other such documents featuring their logo and/or trademark before they go to print. To avoid potential dispute, the contract should contain a provision resolving the issues.

In short, by thinking like an attorney, an event manager can methodically and efficiently review the basic terms of a sponsorship contract. The three-step review provides an event manager with the opportunity to predict a problematic situation, provide for a resolution if it arises, and protect the event by providing for an easy, understandable remedy. Or, putting it another way, the process can avert potential liability for the event and minimize costly lawsuits.

For the sake of convenience, and to help focus an event manager during contract review, liability issues are typically broken down into the following categories:

1. **Trademark issues:**

   a. Sponsor's quality control (i.e., prior approval);
   b. Event's quality control (i.e., prior approval);
   c. Ownership/usage of logos;
   d. Ownership of licensing rights/royalties;
   e. Merchandising rights;
   f. Infringement of trademarks.

2. **Delegation of responsibility (insurance) issues:**

   a. To the observers;
   b. To the participants;

c. To the site;

d. To the innocent bystander;

e. Contractual commitment in the event of rain or other acts of God.

3. **Indemnification:** The protection of each party's rights for a mistake or negligent act committed by the sponsors and/or event; and who is responsible for same.

A well-drafted contract should include a provision concerning each of the above liability issues.

Thinking like an attorney forces an event manager to review the basic terms of a sponsorship agreement and brainstorm for potential areas of dispute. In the long run, these precautionary steps will eliminate many problems. While a contract can never be made dispute-free, the second step to drafting a contract will again minimize those problems.

The third and final step to drafting a contract is to take your draft and convert it into the proper format, structuring the document to physically look like a contract, and adding the appropriate boilerplate provisions.

STEP 3

Most of the provisions discussed in this part are termed "boilerplate." Boilerplate provisions are those clauses that have become standard in all contracts. An event manager must examine each and every provision carefully to determine whether a boilerplate provision applies to a particular agreement and, if so, how that provision should be crafted to ensure a proper fit.

Of course, if all the provisions discussed in the remainder of this article are included in your contract, there will be little room left for the basic terms of the deal. An event manager, therefore, must use his/her judgment to determine whether a particular type of provision is appropriate.

Termination

Provisions regarding termination of a contract require special attention, lest there be room to argue that rights and obligations that should survive termination have been terminated. Use language similar to the following:

> "This agreement will remain in effect until (date). Termination will be without prejudice to the rights and obligations of the parties accrued to the date of termination and following termination of this agreement will continue to apply to, and the Fees due under paragraph ____ will be payable with respect to 1) any contract signed on or prior to termination, and 2) any contract signed after termination on which we were working prior to termination or which is with a party we introduced prior to termination."

Assignment

161

As a general rule, parties to a contract do not want to deal with anyone else but the parties contracted with. To ensure that relationship, the following language might be used:

> "Neither party may transfer or assign any of its rights or obligations under this agreement without the prior written consent of the other. In the case of any transfer or assignment permitted in this paragraph, the transferor shall remain liable for the performance of all obligations under this agreement, regardless of whether those obligations arose before or after the transfer or assignment."

Governing law

Almost every contract defines the law and state where litigation shall take place:

> "This agreement shall be governed by and construed in accordance with the law of the State of _____. All actions, suits or other legal proceedings shall be brought within the City of _____ and State of _____."

Notices

> "Notice, and other communications under this agreement, shall be in writing and sent to each party at its address as set forth in this agreement, unless otherwise agreed in writing prior thereto. Notice will be deemed given on receipt."

Amendment

Amendments should always be in writing:

> "This agreement may be amended only by an instrument in writing signed by the parties hereto."

Waiver

Requiring that waivers be in writing is another mandatory provision.

> "Neither party may waive any of its rights or any obligations of the other party or any provision of this agreement except by an instrument in writing signed by that party."

Integration clauses

This clause provides that the contract at hand supersedes all prior dealings relating to the contract:

> "This agreement contains the entire understanding of the parties with respect to the subject matter of the agreement, and it supersedes all prior understandings and agreements, whether written or oral, and all prior dealings of the parties with respect to the subject matter hereof."

Arbitration vs. Court System

A determination should be made as to whether to include an arbitration provision or not. As a general rule "shallow pockets" (i.e., people with less money) prefer arbitration, and "deep pockets" prefer the courts. There is no right answer; instead, it is a function of timing, cost and the speed of the result that leads most to choose arbitration.

> "Any dispute or claim arising under or with respect to this agreement will be resolved by arbitration in (insert state) in accordance with the Rules of the American Arbitration Association. The decision or award of the arbitrator shall be final and binding upon the parties. Any arbital award may be entered in any court of competent jurisdiction."

Form of the Contract

Finally, after all these concepts, provision, and drafting tips are utilized, you will end up with nothing more than a lot of words on paper. Your task will then be to organize the words into a contract. Is this difficult? No! Make the contract into a simple letter with clear headings so it is easy to read. Use the following form:

Sponsor
Address
City, State

Dear _____:

This will confirm the terms and conditions on which (name of sponsor) has agreed to sponsor the (name of the event) organized by (name of organizer):

(Insert basic terms {discussed in Intro and Step 1}, liability provisions {discussed in Step 2}, and boilerplate provisions {discussed in Step 3}).

If this letter accurately sets forth our agreement, please sign below and return a signed copy to me.

Sincerely,   Agreed and accepted by sponsors on

Event Organizer   this _____ day of 200_

                                              _____

Conclusion

This primer does not cover every provision of a complete well-drafted agreement. All agreements have very individualized characteristics that make each case exceptional. It is therefore strongly recommended that these provisions be clearly understood and skillfully drafted. In all cases, it is wise to consult an attorney. Clearly, if all the suggested steps are followed, an attorney's work will be minimal and the cost will be too. (See Appendix C for sample contract)

Chapter 64 – SPONSOR CONTRACT CHECKLIST

Sponsorship Rights

1. **Sponsor's Official Status**
   - As only sponsor?
   - As only sponsor in a category?
   - Right to veto other sponsors for reasons of incompatibility?
   - Any conflicts with official suppliers?
   - What about sponsorships at other sites or related events?

2. **Signs At The Event**
   - How many?
   - What is the size and placement of sponsor's name relative to others?
   - Who pays?
   - Distance from other's signs?
   - Sign on curtain?
   - Billing on marquees?
   - Signs on vehicles (sound trucks, courtesy cars, etc.)?
   - Any conflicts with permanent signage or arena suppliers?

3. **Advertising Credits**
   - On stationery?
   - In name of event?
   - On program cover?
   - In program advertisement?
   - In all advertising?
   - In all print advertising only?
   - In television advertising?
   - On souvenirs (T-shirts, bumper stickers, etc.)?
   - In press releases?
   - On billboards?
   - On radio?

4. **Sponsorship Fee**
   - How paid?
   - When paid?
   - Secured by letter of credit or escrow?
   - Refundable if television ratings are poor?
   - Exclusivity?

5. **Trademarks**
   - Sponsor's quality control;
   - Promoter's quality control;
   - Ownership of special logos;
   - License/Royalties/Merchandising.

6. **Liabilities**
   - To observers;
   - To participants;
   - To the site;
   - To innocent bystanders;
   - For infringement of trademarks;
   - For contractual commitments in the event of rain, broadcast interruption, force majeure events.

7. **Miscellaneous Topics**
   - Term;
   - Confidentiality;
   - Insurance;
   - Arbitration/Court;
   - Best Efforts Clause;
   - Modifications/Amendments;
   - Ambush;
   - Boilerplate Clauses.

8. **Merchandising Rights**
   - Can the sponsor sell T-shirts, mugs, similar souvenirs?
   - Can the sponsor manufacture its own souvenirs or buy from the promoter at cost?
   - Who gets the profit on merchandising efforts?

9. **Ownership of Television Rights**
   - Who owns and controls?
   - If the promoter owns, does the sponsor have right of first refusal on available spots?
   - Is there an estimated rating and/or a rebate for low ratings?
   - Does the sponsor get opening/closing credits or billboards?
   - Does the sponsor have rights to use footage of the event for current and/or future advertising?
   - Will the Promoter get all rights necessary from participants to allow use of clips in commercials without further compensation?

10. **Public Relations and Personal Appearances**
    - Can the promoter commit key personnel or talent to personal appearances on behalf of the sponsor?
    - Can the promoter commit its spokespeople to mention the sponsor's name whenever possible?
    - Does the sponsor have the right to erect a courtesy tent?
    - Can the promoter commit the key personnel participating in an event to attending post-event parties in their honor?
    - Does the sponsor get free tickets (for key customers, tie-in contests, etc.)?

11. **Future Options**
    - Does the sponsor have the right to renew its sponsorship on the same terms and conditions (plus a fixed increase in the price)?
    - Does the sponsor have the right of first refusal for subsequent years?

Common Contract Clauses

1. Termination;
2. Assignment;
3. Governing Law;
4. Arbitration;
5. Notice;
6. Execution and Counterparts;
7. Authority to Contract and to Sign;
8. Amendment;
9. Waiver;
10. Delay in Enforcing Rights;
11. Remedies;
12. Integration Clauses;
13. Expenses and Interests;
14. Indemnities;
15. Severability;
16. Section Headings;
17. Definitions and Preamble.

Contact a lawyer for exact wording for these clauses.

Chapter 65 – SIGNATURES: HOW TO PROPERLY SIGN A DOCUMENT

Sometimes it seems as if we sign our life away. Sponsorship contracts, vendor agreements, insurance and loan documents and much, much more. Sooner or later, in the event management industry, documents such as these cross our desk for signature.

How you sign these documents is very important. But, before I explain why, how many of you have done the following: A promissory note or loan document requires your signature in order for a **corporate** line of credit to be issued. After review of the document and verification of the terms, you sign on the dotted line ... no more, no less.

Well, take note. That simple, innocent act may have actually signed your life away. In other words, such an act may have created your own personal liability for that corporate debt.

New York case discussed this unusual legal scenario. <u>Level Line V. Balzano</u>, Kings County, 1992. In the case, the plaintiff sued the president of a company in his individual capacity based on the fact that the president signed a loan document in his name only, not on behalf of the corporation. The president, of course, claimed his intent was to sign on the behalf of the corporation. The court, unfortunately, found in favor of plaintiff stating that the president's signature ***did not note his official capacity*** (e.g. "John Doe", President). In short, the president was held personally liable for the debt

What does this case represent? It represents a simple lesson for all corporate officers and employees that sign contracts. The lesson - <u>Always execute documents in your capacity as an officer or employee</u> rather than simply stating your name. While very few "unidentified" signatures may lead to your own personal liability, it is better to be safe than sorry. To avoid such a problem, one simple rule of safety is suggested. Sign every corporate document in the following manner:

XYZ CORPORATION

By_____

    Name, Title

If the document only has a signature line, then write in the remaining information. One thing is for sure: This simple procedure will eliminate the potential for your own personal liability on a Corporation document, which no smart businessperson, can afford. No one can, or will, mistake the intent behind your signature if you follow this suggestion.

Chapter 66 – UNDERSTANDING THE DIFFERENCE: OPTIONS TO RENEW VS. RIGHT OF FIRST REFUSAL

There are two simple, but important, sponsorship terms -- The Option to Renew and The Right of First Refusal - that are provisions found in almost every sponsorship contract, whether used separately or in conjunction with each other.

Option to Renew:

Definition: The option to renew gives the existing sponsor the sole option to extend the sponsorship agreement when the initial term of the contract expires.

Sample Language: Organizer hereby grants to sponsor the right to renew its sponsorship hereunder on the same terms and conditions as contained herein (except the sponsorship fee described in paragraph ___ shall be $_____ and shall be paid on a mutually agreeable schedule similar to the one set forth in paragraph ____. *) Sponsor shall exercise said option, if at all, by giving organizer written notice thereof within **(insert #)** days of the expiration of the term of this Agreement. In the event that sponsor does not exercise such option, the terms of the sponsorship agreement shall terminate upon the expiration of that option period.

*Note: The insert in the above paragraph is typically a dollar amount slightly higher than that of the original sponsorship fee (a fixed, agreed upon increase).

Comments: The right to renew has an attractive value to sponsors. This is particularly true for new or first time events. Why? For their risks, the sponsors get a fixed increase in the sponsorship fee for the following year's event and future events.

To be enforceable, however, please note the option language must contain an offer, a specific time period in which the option must be exercised and valuable consideration given to the event granting the option.

Advantage: Organizer has another tangible value to offer a sponsor. It also gives the sponsor a feeling of security -- meaning, if the event is successful, the sponsor cannot be squeezed out by competitors.

Disadvantage: The one danger behind such a provision is that a sponsor should not be given an unlimited right to renew. The organizer should limit the option to a specific number of years. An event should always be prepared for success. If the event is a success, the value of future sponsorships should not be restricted but, rather, be left to the market for determination.

As always, a contract is a "give and take" situation; know your options and be prepared!

Right of First Refusal:

Definition: The Right of First Refusal allows a window of opportunity for the existing sponsor to make an offer to retain his/her sponsorship right to an event.

Sample Language: Upon the expiration of this agreement, organizer agrees that it will not accept and/or contract with another sponsor for the same sponsorship category at issue for a period of **(insert #)** months, without first giving sponsor, in writing, an opportunity to accept and/or contract with the organizer on substantially similar terms. If sponsor matches the terms of the other sponsor's offer, organizer agrees to enter into agreement with sponsor on such terms.

Upon receipt of written notice from organizer concerning other potential sponsorship offers, sponsor shall have 30 days to exercise its right of first refusal. If sponsor elects to exercise this right within the time frame specified, it shall notify sponsor in writing of its intentions.

Comments: This clause allows an event producer to accept the sponsor's offer or find an offer of greater value. A lower offer cannot be accepted.

Advantage: The true advantage is to sponsor. It allows the sponsor to walk away from negotiations with an option to match any competitor's offer. The advantage to an organizer is that it allows the market to set the price. The advantage to the sponsor is limited by the window of opportunity. Such a clause should restrict the period in which a sponsor has to match the offer and the scope in which the terms can be matched.

Disadvantage: As a practical matter, when an organizer has given such a clause to a sponsor, it can be difficult to interest new sponsors. Why should Nike spend time negotiating the terms of the deal, only to have the deal supplanted at the last moment by Reebok with its right of first refusal? To the organizer, such clauses discourage new sponsors.

Chapter 67 – KEEP YOUR IDEAS SAFE

Rubik's Cube, Mutant Ninja Turtles, the New York City Marathon and the Special Olympics.

What do these four items have in common? Answer: Each is an original idea.

Imagine if you had a sure-fire, once-in-a-lifetime, original idea - an idea to create, for example, an event to promote something such as sandcastle building. Like most great ideas, money is the first and last shortcoming to getting the project started. Money is typically needed to produce, manufacture, promote and/or sell the idea. Money most inventors or creators, unfortunately, do not have.

As such, ideas are usually needed to be shared with others, in order to attract financing or to develop the appropriate channels for marketing, manufacturing or promotions.

It is at this moment that most inventors or creators fail to realize that a new idea is like new property: it can be possessed by whoever discovers it. To those unknowing inventors, it is at the financing and development stage that most ideas are unfairly taken or, for that matter, stolen, the inventor being left with no recourse whatsoever.

So you ask what protection does the creator of a new idea have? Good question because a creator's options are limited.

In order to avoid or minimize the chance of such misfortunes, it is suggested that an inventor complete one of the following steps prior to releasing his idea to others:

1. Copyright his inventions; or

2. Enter into a written contract (i.e., confidentiality agreement).

Copyright

Federal copyright laws are frequently used by creators to pursue those alleged to have misappropriated their ideas and used them in motion pictures, merchandise, event productions or any other type of public medium.

To establish a bona fide claim for copyright infringement, the creator of the idea must prove ownership of a valid copyright and that certain elements of the original work were copied.

Copyright protection is, however, limited. While others may not copy an author's original expression of an idea, copyright laws typically allow that anyone may freely use the ideas expressed in the author's work. In practice, the line that separates an "idea" from the "expression" is not easy to locate. Arguably, this creates a very large gray area for the inventor - especially when one is talking about something as intangible as a great idea.

The best way to avoid this confusion is detail. But at the early stages of an idea, detail can be the most difficult thing to provide. Add in the expenses and time to

170

copyright, and it is clear that for most inventors, copyrighting may not be the best available method.

Contract Protection

For most inventors, a written contract can provide the best, most cost-effective security measure available. That is because, even if an abstract idea cannot rise to the levels of copyright "property", its disclosure may be valid consideration for a contract.

A contract relating to an idea is valid (and consideration sufficient) if something of real value is exchanged. For example, if the idea recipient is saved the time, money, or effort of obtaining or developing the idea through other channels or resources, then valid consideration will exist to support the contract at issue.

The following language is suggested for inclusion in any cover letter/contract and "signed off" by the recipient prior to releasing your idea:

1. All information disclosed by creator to **(name of recipient)** that relates or refers, directly or indirectly, to the **(name of idea)** shall be deemed confidential and shall constitute confidential information. Confidential information shall include (a) all documents generated by **(name of recipient)** which contain, comment upon, or relate in any way to any information received from creator; and, (b) any written samples of the **(name of idea)** received from creator together with any information derived by **(name of recipient)** therefrom;

2. Creator will disclose the confidential information to **(name of recipient)** solely for the purpose of allowing **(name of recipient)** to evaluate the **(name of idea)** to determine, in its sole discretion, whether the **(name of idea)** may be further developed into a project;

3. The confidential information shall remain the property of the creator and shall not be disclosed or revealed by **(name of recipient)** to anyone else except its employees who have a need to know the information in connection with **(name of recipient's)** evaluation of the **(name of idea)**;

4. If **(recipient)** determines the **(name of idea)** cannot be further developed into a project, **(recipient)** shall within five (5) business days after such determination return any and all confidential information to creator, along with all copies of the **(name of idea)** or derivatives thereof and all writings generated by **(recipient)** in connection with **(recipient's)** evaluation of the **(name of idea)** or the confidential information; and

5. If **(recipient)** does, however, determine that the **(name of idea)** is suitable for further development into a project, it is agreed that **(recipient)** shall not use the confidential information for any purpose whatsoever other than for the sole purpose permitted in paragraph 2 above, unless and until a further executed agreement is first made between the parties herein setting forth the terms and conditions under which the rights to the **(name of idea)** and the confidential information are licensed to, or acquired by **(recipient)**.

Conclusion

As the preceding analysis demonstrates, there are few rules of law by which an idea creator can be assured of the outcome. However, there are certain precautions, in addition to the contract or copyright steps, that an idea creator can take; all of which increase his/her ability to exercise rights of ownership. Such precautions are:

- The creator should try to express his or her idea in some original manner or form that distinguishes it and the expression of that idea. The less likely that an earlier author has employed a similar expression, the greater likelihood that an author's idea can be seen as property.

- The creator should also forewarn his or her intended recipient of the impending submission and of his expectations concerning the idea being submitted. Such circumstances can assist in establishing the contract (written or oral) and the recipient's knowledge of same, if a dispute arises.

Good luck, be cautious and, with the above information in hand, keep on creating!

Chapter 68 – TRADEMARKS

PART 1: Protecting your event

Whether you realize it or not, everyone sees, uses and makes daily decisions on the basis of trademarks. Coke, NBC's peacock, American Express' slogan "Don't Leave Home Without It," the Five Olympic rings, -- they are all well-known trademarks and are instrumental to their owners in selling their product, service or event. According to most marketing and advertising handbooks, a good trademark is what gives a product its image, public identity and, if recognizable enough, the ability to tell a story to the consumer.

As it specifically pertains to event management, a good, recognizable trademark, such as the logo for the Indianapolis 500, not only creates an identity and recognition for an event, but impacts on attendance and admission prices as well. In short, a name, symbol or tag line that an event uses may well be its single, most valuable asset.

Just as you can own personal property or real estate, you can own, protect and profit from your trademarked creations. The Federal Trademark Act of 1946, commonly known as the Lanham Act, provides for such ownership and protection by dealing with the degree to which the owner of that name or symbol will be afforded a monopoly over the use of that name or symbol. Every promoter, producer, graphic designer or artist involved in, or associated with, event management should at least be familiar with the benefits and financial possibilities afforded by these laws.

If you design or create a mark for your event and want to acquire legal rights to it and use it properly, certain basic steps should be considered:

- **Step 1 - Make sure your mark or symbol qualifies as a trademark.** A trademark may be a word, symbol or combination of words and design, a slogan or even a distinctive sound which identifies and distinguishes the goals or services of one party from those of another. A trademark must be something that is inherently distinctive or that can become distinctive, i.e., Jell-O, Kleenex, Wimbledon or Xerox. As a general rule, generic words and symbols are not inherently distinctive.

- **Step 2 - Make sure you preserve your mark as a trade secret until you use it.** Rights to a trademark are acquired by the actual use of the mark in connection with the sale of goods, services or an event. Therefore, during the developmental stage of your project, you must treat your trademark as a secret so others won't adopt your proposed mark and use it first.

- **Step 3 - Make sure your mark is original.** This step requires a trademark search. This typically is conducted by an attorney or professional search firm. Such a search can minimize the probability that you will not be able to register your mark or will have to change your mark after you have invested a great deal of time, effort and money in developing and marketing your proposed trademarked event. Be smart and avoid unnecessary litigation.

- **Step 4 - Use your trademark.** The first to use a mark or symbol in conjunction with the sale of it product, service or event, owns the trademark and acquires the right to protect it against others. It's important to understand that Federal registration is not required to establish rights to a mark, nor is it required to begin use of a mark. Use of the mark in connection with the sale of your product, service or event is sufficient by itself.

- **Step 5 - Register your trademark.** Federal registration of your trademark, however, is strongly recommended because of the additional protection it affords. The advantages are several: a) once your mark is registered, that registration is constructive notice to everyone of your prior ownership and use of that mark; b) having a Federal registration of your mark entitles you to commence a lawsuit for infringement in Federal Court, and c) your registration prevents others from registering confusing, similar marks. To register a trademark in your state, call or write to the Secretary of State in your state's capitol. Ask for a trademark application form and instructions. To register it federally, write to the Patent and Trademark Office, Washington, DC 20231 for an application.

- **Step 6 - Use your trademark properly.** Once a Federal registration is issued, the registrant should give notice to the public by using the ®symbol or the phrase "Registered in U.S. Patent Trademark Office" or Reg. U.S. Pat. & Tm. Off. It's very important to use a trademark properly and to continually police misuse of your trademark by others. Otherwise, the privileges associated with the trademark, even though they are registered "forever," can be lost.

For further information about trademarks, you can call 703-308-HELP for a booklet entitled *Basic Facts About Registering a Trademark.* Keep in mind any trademarks may have individual characteristics that make it exceptional and, in most cases, it may be wise to consult an attorney.

PART 2: Licensing

Finding additional sources of income are always important to an event coordinator. Due to the competitiveness of today's marketplace, the success of a particular event is ultimately judged by the revenue it generates.

If event coordinators find this to be the case, then please take note. Consider this possible solution: a relatively low cost, low risk way to build on the existing equity of your event and, of course, add dollars to your budget with a well designed trademark licensing program.

Trademark licensing, the granting to others the right to use your trademark or trade name in their business, has become one of the fastest growing business activities in the world. The recent "boom" in trademark licensing has taken names and likenesses of Harry Potter, Michael Jordan, the Rolling Stones and even Fred Flintstone into every room and closet of the American home.

The possibilities for licensing an event are without limits. Events such as The America's Cup, the World Series, Indianapolis 500 and Wimbledon are already successfully licensed. By simply utilizing an event's assets, an event coordinator not only capitalizes on the public's recognition of its name and logo, but can generate revenue for the event at the same time. As research indicates, "the sheer visibility of a successful, coordinated licensing program is a strong enticement to attracting additional advertisers." As such, an effective licensing program may be the ultimate marketing strategy for your event.

In order to create such a program, an enormous amount of preliminary work must first be accomplished. Arguably, at least to some degree, the bottom-line success of a licensing program depends on decisions made, or not made, at the start of the program. The following comments address the basic introductory concepts an organization must consider before developing a trademark licensing program.

A. **The trademark**

The most basic element of a trademark licensing program is the trademark itself. An event must have clear title and ownership of a name or mark in order to license it. This mark can be the name of the event or some word or design that has been created to represent the event.

While usage is the foundation for ownership of trademark rights, such rights do not necessarily provide protection to the owner when used on products (i.e., T-shirts, cups, etc.). Therefore, it's strongly suggested that protecting your event's name on a product is best accomplished through Federal registration of that trademark.

B. **Fame and fortune**

Having an eye-catching trademark is also not enough to start a licensing program. Certain other intangibles are needed, namely "Fame and Fortune."

Fame, prestige or the uniqueness of the event can provide the basis for a licensing program. Every event has its area of influence, its fans and its participants, which may lend itself to a particular product or line of products (i.e., Wisconsin Cheeseheads). As such, event coordinators must carefully analyze the characteristics of the people that attend their event before manufacturing a licensed product.

In addition, a typical licensing program needs substantial investment (or fortune) from either the licensor (the event) or the licensee (the manufacturer) to make it successful. For most events, this investment has already been made and continues to be made in a variety of ways (i.e., media attention and event promotions). Certainly, if an event has no recognizable value, a licensing program would be useless.

C. **Product application**

The third element requires that the trademark (and event's reputation) be successfully applied as a name, logo or seal to the most appropriate commercial licensing product available. There are many obvious products, such as caps or key chains, that appeal to event attendees.

D. Resources and commitment

Finally, a trademark licensing program will not be successful without the resources and commitment of your event staff. It requires careful management and administration. In fact, the monitoring and protection of your trademark not only requires attention and expense but, more importantly, it serves to safeguard the reputation of your event. Remember, your event name and logo are your property, so make sure you protect them.

While a trademark licensing program is a relatively simple idea, there are many potential dangers that can damage a licensing program and quite possibly harm the reputation of your event. Thus, even though the possibility for success is great, it is urged that a thorough, careful examination of these basic concepts be considered first. The bottom line success of a licensing program depends on the decisions made, or not made, at the start of the program.

PART 3 - Building Successful Licensing Programs

Although the concepts behind a trademark licensing program are simple, not all are successful. Why? Because the key to success lies in the planning, preparation and research each event promoter puts forth at the start of the program.

Studies repeatedly indicate that the failure of a licensing program generally can be traced back to the same reason -- a combination of inexperience and insufficient planning. It therefore seems apparent that in order to avoid these pitfalls, a licensing program must start with a solid foundation, including a well-conceived business plan and a well-drafted licensing agreement. This article addresses drafting the licensing agreement only.

To put the importance of a licensing agreement in the proper perspective, it's commonly acknowledged that although the "trademark" is the property upon which the licensing program is built, it's the agreement itself that's both the foundation and the framework of the program. The agreement is the foundation because it defines the parties involved, the responsibilities between these parties and the means and method of operation for the licensing program. In short, the agreement structures a relationship between the licenser (event) and the licensee (manufacturer). It also establishes the specific terms of the program, such as royalty payments, the products to be licensed and the particular usage of the event's trademarks.

As Martin Greenberg, author of *Sports Law Practice*, aptly states, "The engine which drives any merchandise licensing machine is the licensing agreement." Therefore, the importance of a well-drafted licensing agreement can't be over-emphasized. The following provides a brief primer for event promoters on the importance of a licensing agreement.

License grant clause

The grant clause delineates the basic rights the event is granting to the manufacturer. This is the portion of the agreement that actually assigns to the licensee the right to use an event's trademark and permits the licensee to use its name, design or likeness in conjunction with the trademark. To event promoters, this provision is what legally allows the use of your event name and logo to be applied to the manufacturing, distribution, promotion, advertising and sale of licensed products.

Frequently this clause also defines whether the license being issued is exclusive or non-exclusive. Under an exclusive license, the event typically grants to the licensee all rights to make, use and sell the licensed trademark and retains "one thing ownership" of the trademark. A non-exclusive agreement allows the event to grant any number of licenses to its trademarks that it wishes.

Licensed marks/licensed products

Trademarks to be licensed should be clearly identified and included as a schedule attached to the license agreement. In fact, the definition section of the license agreement must contain language which incorporates the marks identified in the schedule. Similarly, the products to be licensed and distributed by the manufacturer should be clearly identified and listed as a schedule to the agreement.

It's necessary to define the products to be licensed to prevent the licensee from arbitrarily selling your trademark. Remember, control your mark and supervise your property. This is the only way to safeguard the reputation of the event and to make sure that your licensing program makes money.

Accounts and reporting

A license agreement must require the licensee to maintain complete and accurate records and accounts covering all transactions. Record-keeping and reporting of sales are typically done on a quarterly basis.

The agreement should, in fact, permit the event promoter to inspect and audit, at any time upon notice, the books and records of the licensee. Regular, routine audits of a licensee based on random samples of product will put a licensee on notice that you are serious about your event licensing program. If nothing more, audits and inspections will give a licensee incentive to keep accurate records and properly report sales.

Quality controls

Licensed merchandise is a reflection of your event so supervise it carefully. As such, the agreement should contain language requiring the licensee, before selling or distributing any product, to furnish the event (at no charge) samples of the licensed product. In addition, the event promoter should include language directing the licensee to submit all samples of advertising, point-of-sale display, catalogues, sales sheets and other items that display or picture the event logo for approval prior to production.

Methods for termination

Include a revocation clause in the agreement that allows the event to cancel the agreement for non-performance or for breach. Termination language should also contain provisions requiring the licensee to itemize his inventory at the time of termination and permit the manufacturer to sell the remaining inventory for three to six months after termination subject to normal royalty terms. At the end of this disposal period, the agreement should require the licensee to destroy, or turn over to the event, any leftover inventory.

Modification and waiver

Similarly, the license agreement should always include a provision that permits the agreement to be amended with consent of the parties. Changes will occur in the business relationship, product line, licensed territory, the trademarks or even the royalty rate, all of which can impact the agreement. If not provided for, it means the termination of the current licensing agreement and renegotiation of a new agreement.

Royalties

The royalty clause defines the amount of compensation to be received by the event as a result of the licensing agreement. This provision directly reflects the skill and negotiating ability of the event promoter. The stature of the event, the nature of the competition and the potential market should all be taken into account in determining the royalty rate. Typically, this rate falls between 7% and 9% of the wholesale price of the licensed product.

Structuring of royalty provisions can take on a number of variations. The more common style, in addition to straight percentage, is as follows:

a. A guaranteed minimum royalty payment during the term of the agreement coupled with royalties based on a percentage of the net sales;

b. An advance payment up front to be credited against a minimum guaranteed payment; and

c. Compensation where the licensee pays the event promoter a guaranteed minimum, regardless of sales. The minimum payment is the offset against the percentage of compensation owed.

In any case, a promoter must be absolutely sure that the agreement includes a clear definition of how the "wholesale price", upon which the royalties will be based, is calculated to prevent disagreements from arising at a later date.

Conclusion

Remember that the preceding focuses on certain provisions an event promoter should be aware of. This primer doesn't cover every provision of a complete, well-drafted licensing agreement. Licensing agreements have very individualized characteristics that make each case exceptional. Nonetheless, it's recommended that these provisions be clearly understood, carefully controlled and skillfully negotiated. In all cases, it's wise to consult with an attorney.

Chapter 69 – RISK MANAGEMENT - MINIMIZING LIABILITY

Event managers cannot depend upon the court system to protect their event from lawsuits. Sooner or later, whether it is deserving or not, your event will be the subject of a lawsuit. Do not, however, wait for that day to come. At that point, it is too late to take any preventive action. Instead, take positive, affirmative steps to decrease the risk of lawsuit before it happens by becoming aware of those situations which may give rise to negligent activity.

In other words, create a risk management plan. A risk management plan is a defensive strategy that identifies, evaluates and controls loss to property, clients, employees and the public. The bottom line is - a successful plan minimizes loss and decreases liability.

While there are a variety of steps involved in completing a total risk management plan for your event, there are a number of simple and basic steps that can be taken to protect any event and immediately reduce the potential for lawsuit as follows.

Waiver of Liability

An event manager may request participants to execute a waiver or disclaimer of liability. If a participant executes such an agreement, he/she agrees to (1) accept the risk of harm arising from another's conduct, (2) relieve the event of all responsibility for such safety, and (3) forego any lawsuit against the event if there is an injury as a result of the event's negligence. It is also wise to include the specific sponsors of the event in the waiver statement.

Four elements are necessary for a court to legally enforce a participant waiver statement against an adult:

(1) The document must be clean and not ambiguous;

(2) It must be signed voluntarily and in absence of fraud;

(3) The event must not be subject to a positive duty imposed by law; and

(4) Exoneration of the event and its sponsors against whom negligence is charged will not adversely affect the public interest of the state.

The following is an example of a waiver statement that has been used successfully to prevent liability:

"I understand that there may be some risk involved in my participation in the above sporting activity, including, but not limited to, those associated with weather conditions, playing conditions, equipment and other participants.

I fully assume the risk associated with the participation in said sporting activity.

I hereby waive any and all claims that I may have against **(the event and its sponsors),** its directors, officers, supervisors, umpires, referees or other employees or

179

agents arising out of any personal injury or property damage that is incurred during said anticipation, whether active or inactive."

Liability Insurance

In addition to obtaining waivers, the event should negotiate for liability insurance. The event must be insured against such risks, but it also is politically correct to name sponsors, the municipality, the owner of the venue, etc., as additional insureds on the liability policy as well. At a minimum, insurance protects against unforeseen and expensive litigation costs. At best, it may save the life of your event.

Preventive Management

Notwithstanding the above suggestions, the easiest and most common sense defense strategy is to think ahead and plan for those situations. Remember, think like an attorney - Predict, Provide and Protect. The checklist referenced below is an example of what should be incorporated into a sporting events planning and preparation stages. Event managers should:

1. Inspect the playing surface for visible hazards;

2. Be sure the weather conditions are appropriate to begin and continue the event. It is better to err on the side of safety when it comes to weather and participants;

3. Inspect the game equipment;

4. Inspect the equipment of the participants;

5. Enforce the rules of the sport to maintain proper control;

6. Be sure authorized personnel and visitors are at a safe distance from the area of play;

7. Deal properly with potential and actual participant injury. When a participant appears to be injured, you should take the following steps:

    •Stop the contest as soon as possible;

    •Report the injury to all appropriate personnel;

    •Don't touch, move or assist in moving the injured party without the direction of licensed medical staff;

    •Do not resume the activity until the injured participant is pronounced ready to play by medical personnel or has been removed from the playing surface;

    •Be patient - in some situations you may have to wait for medical attention to arrive and attend to the injured participant.

8. If you temporarily stop the activity for any problem, be sure the problem is satisfactorily corrected before resuming play; and

9. Be aware of potential problems which may develop throughout the course of an event and deal with them with the same reasoned judgment you would use to run the entire event, erring always on the side of safety.

The golden rule for event managers in the area of risk management is plan thoroughly, check and recheck the execution of the event, think with common sense each step of the way and provide for those situations that could go awry. As always, common sense and some forethought go a long way to saving the event money and making its production a success. For the overall health of your event, avoid lawsuits!!!

Chapter 70 – AMBUSH MARKETING

Sponsorship is based on perception. Event managers perceive value based upon the number of participants and spectators that attend. Corporations perceive value based upon the "so-called" image enhancement and audience awareness associated with an event. Either way, the value perceived, for lack of a better expression, is in "the eye of the beholder." And, that perceived value, large or small, retains its worth *only* if a corporation and/or an event can protect and maintain their perception of that sponsorship opportunity.

Now, take a moment to imagine what could happen if another corporation could obtain sponsorship value without the cost. Certainly, it is easy to see that such a happening could destroy any perceived value associated with an event, causing an event manager the worst possible nightmare ... SPONSORSHIP CHAOS. After the obvious yelling and screaming from your paying corporate sponsors subsides, the real problem still remains for an event: How can I create a value if it is possible for a company to get the same value without the cost?

Welcome to a common problem associated with sponsorships - **Ambush Marketing (sometimes called parasitic marketing).** Whether it be the Super Bowl, the Indy 500, the Olympic Games, or a local road race, chances are you will find some evidence of ambush marketing at work. One classic example was found at the Summer Olympic Games. Reebok was the official shoe of the games for a $40,000,000.00 fee. Nike, however, created a situation that confused many attendees as to who the official shoe was. Without paying the requisite fee, Nike built a theme park just outside the Olympic Village and hired many of the notable Olympians to participate in their marketing campaign - all rights and properties outside the legal control of the Olympic management. To the eye of the spectator, it was just not clear who the official shoe sponsor was. The value of Reebok's sponsorship was destroyed. In short, Reebok was ambushed by Nike, damaging Reebok's perception in the Games, and affecting any future business relationship with the International Olympic Committee.

Such underhanded tactics are not limited to high profile events. Ambush marketing can, unfortunately, arise wherever successful marketing opportunities exist - meaning, ambush marketing can attack any event, including yours. It is therefore important for all event managers to understand the concept of ambush marketing and how to minimize its chances of occurring.

So, you ask, what is the technical definition? According to most sources, ambush marketing is a concept that describes the actions of companies who aggressively seek to associate themselves with a sponsored event without paying the requisite fee. The ambush occurs by giving the impression to consumers that the ambusher (such as Nike in the previous example) is actually an official sponsor or is somehow affiliated with the event - when, in fact, the ambusher has no relation to that event at all. Such marketing practices provide the benefits of a legitimate, paid-for sponsorship at no cost. Moreover, it destroys any perceived value an event may have, impacts terribly on the paying sponsor's rights and, most important to any marketing campaign, causes

182

confusion to the consumer. Indeed, when all is said and done, ambush marketing creates a deadly question for event managers to answer to its paying sponsors: Why pay for something I can get for free?

While ambush marketing can never be completely eliminated from an event, there are several practices an event manager and sponsor can adopt which will improve their chances against being ambushed. The following four practices are suggested:

1. Event organizers must make sure they have effectively protected, usually via trademark registration, the logos, symbols, and other visual identifiers associated with their event. In other words, make it difficult for a non-paying party to utilize your marks. This is the easiest way for a non-paying corporation to associate itself. If you do not own your symbols, it is possible for anyone to use them in their advertising or marketing campaigns.

2. Event managers should also tightly control, through the use of written contracts, the sale of souvenirs and signage, *both at the site and around the location of the event.* A non-paying corporation cannot steal the spotlight from being associated with your event, if the opportunity does not exist. So, look into how you can control the advertising opportunities not only within the confines of your venue, but the surrounding areas as well.

3. Take advantage of all the opportunities afforded by a particular sponsorship agreement. Use all aspects of the inventory offered by the event. By filling the perceived voids, there is less opportunity for a potential ambusher to capture the paying sponsor's marketing niche.

4. Event management and sponsoring corporations should also establish provisions and procedures allowing for enforcement, by the courts, of the proprietary rights, in general, and the particular rights granted under a sponsorship agreement. An event must protect its sponsor's rights. If nothing else, it helps secure the relationship and shows a corporation you care about them. Also, do not take legal action lightly. If ambushers realize you are willing to fight, they are less likely to attack. Remember, part of the beauty of ambush marketing is the limited cost; if you create an expense, the ambusher may look for other, more cost-effective opportunities.

It is well know that sponsorship is currently big business. It is also a well-known fact that the bigger the business, the bigger the prize (i.e., money and recognition). So, it is not surprising that where successful marketing, promotional and advertising opportunities exist, an aggressive competitor may resort to ambush tactics in order to be associated with an event. Because there are so many possibilities for an ambusher to exploit, it is unlikely that an event or sponsor can anticipate all ambush marketing attacks in advance. Indeed, ambush marketing, if properly executed, will more often than not, be very difficult to prevent. As seen above, even the Olympics have a very difficult time with these tactics.

Attention to the general points previously raised can help assure your paying sponsors' rights are protected and help establish a strong foundation for asserting an event's rights against ambushers. Remember, sponsorship is based on perceived value. If you cannot protect that value, then eventually there will be no sellable value associated with your event. If, however, you remain aware of ambush marketing and are willing to fight it to the best of your event's ability, then it is possible for you to at least control the damage it can do to the marketing of your event.

Chapter 71 – PROTECTING AGAINST RISK - BUYING THE RIGHT KIND OF INSURANCE

What do the promoters of the Super Bowl, a car owner and your employer have in common? Don't know the answer? Then let me give you a clue. Each owns some type of "risk prevention" service. Now, do you know? No, it is not a "hi-tech" security system. And it is certainly not a spare tire. So, what is it you ask? Simple, it is insurance. Whether it be a general liability policy or worker's compensation, one thing is certain - the employer, the car owner and the promoter own insurance.

But, what exactly is insurance? Grolier's Electronic Encyclopedia defines insurance as "a mechanism for reducing financial risk and spreading financial loss." Therefore, an insurance company makes a profit by investing in risk. A mathematical determination is made by the company as to the occurrence of the risk and, based on that risk, the company charges a "premium" to guarantee against its occurrence. The document issued by the company discussing these terms is called an "insurance policy." If the risk does not occur, the company keeps the premium. If, however, the risk occurs, the insurance company pays for a certain amount of the loss caused by that risk ("policy limits"). To a businessperson, a homeowner or anyone who wants to protect their assets, the purchase of an insurance policy is a means of security - a safety blanket of sorts.

In the United States, since the Revolutionary War, some 6,000 insurance companies collect well in excess of $200 billion in annual premiums, employ more than 2 million people, and hold assets valued at close to $800 billion. Based on these numbers, it is safe to say that insurance companies will issue policies to protect against any risk; even event management related risks. But because event promoters are exposed to risk on a variety of levels (i.e. general liability, worker's compensation, errors and omissions), there unfortunately is not just one policy to purchase. Depending on the size and scope of the event, there may be several different policies that have to be considered. The rest of this chapter briefly reviews some of the forms of insurance available to event promoters:

Comprehensive General Liability Policy (Commercial Liability Policy)

This standard policy provides that an insurance company will defend your event against any suit and pay any damages that your event is liable to pay because of bodily injury or property damage caused by an "occurrence." An "occurrence" is typically defined as an "accident, including continuous or repeated exposure to conditions, which results in bodily injury or property damage neither expected nor intended from the standpoint of the insured." If the event promoter desires, the policy can cover spectators, participants and other parties. Of course, the more parties the policy insures, the greater the risk and the higher the premium.

185

Professional Liability Policy/Malpractice Policy/Errors and Omissions Policy

This policy protects an event promoter from lawsuits that occur as a result of his or her "failure to use due care and the degree of skill expected" of a professional. In other words, this policy is a safety net against errors or omissions in judgment that occur during the management of an event.

Personal and Advertising Injury Liability

This policy protects an event against lawsuits based on the invasion of a person's privacy, slander, copyright and/or plagiarism.

Worker's Compensation/Employer's Liability Insurance

This policy, which is usually required by statute, protects an event against lawsuits that occur to its employees, whether it be personal injury or injury to property.

There are also insurance policies that speak for themselves: liquor liability insurance, broadcast interruption insurance for pay-per-view events and business interruption insurance. There are also policies that guarantee an event will take place (usually required by a sponsor or local government) called contract bonds or performance/payment bonds. Such bonds guarantee that the work or, in this case, the event, will be performed as planned.

As one can see, insurance is available in a variety of forms and provides a variety of protections. Events, due to all the obvious risk factors, clearly need such protection. As such, an event promoter should locate, and come to trust, an insurance broker. The broker can identify your risks, help estimate your exposure, and assess the limits of protection your event needs. Insurance should ultimately become, if it has not already, a line item cost in every event's budget. But like all event budgets, the cost of this protection should be carefully scrutinized and analyzed to gain the maximum protection for the minimum cost.

The right insurance issued in conjunction with a good risk management program means a safe, well-executed event will occur and, best of all, your expected bottom line profits will result.

Chapter 72 – GOOD NEWS, NONPROFITS; CORPORATE SPONSORSHIP PROTECTION IS HERE!

Good news! The rules of the sponsorship game have changed. Through the hard work and lobbying efforts of nonprofit organizations, bowl games, Olympic sports committees, and the art community, the battle over corporate sponsorship payments has been won. On August 5, 1997, President Clinton signed into law the Taxpayers Relief Act of 1997. In one quick moment, years of dispute over the taxability of corporate sponsorship payments to nonprofit events was resolved -- and most unbelievably resolved in favor of the nonprofit and its corporate sponsors. In simple language, the Taxpayers Relief Act of 1997 effectively exempts most sponsorship income from the 33% unrelated business income tax (UBIT) which a 501 (c) 3 nonprofit might otherwise be forced to pay.

What this law did was to provide a corporate sponsorship provision that distinguished between **"qualified sponsorship payments"** (not subject to UBIT) and payments made to tax exempt organizations in return for **advertising** the sponsor's products or services (subject to UBIT). To those who are paying attention, it is therefore quite clear that, in order to avoid taxation, nonprofits and corporate sponsors need to make sure their sponsorship arrangements fall within the definition of a **"qualified sponsor payment."**

Under the new law, a **"qualified sponsor payment"** is specifically defined as "...any payment made by an individual or entity engaged in trade or business where there is no arrangement or expectation that the sponsor will receive any substantial return benefit other than the use or acknowledgment of the sponsor's name, logo and/or product lines in connection with the activities of the tax exempt organization that receives the payment." Simply stated, the **"qualified sponsorship payment"** hinges upon the event's **acknowledgment** of a corporation's support and paid advertising.

Non-Taxable

According to the **NCAA News** and the **IFEA Legislative Update**'s interpretation, permissible corporate "acknowledgments" at an event are categorized as follows:

- Sponsor logos that do not contain a comparative or qualitative description of a sponsor's product, services, facilities or companies;
- The identification of a sponsor's locations/addresses and telephone numbers;
- Value-neutral descriptions, including displays or visual depictions of a sponsor's product line or services; and
- The identification of a sponsor brand or trade name and product or service listings.

Taxable

Conversely, these same sources highlight advertising benefits similar to the examples listed below **as taxable**:

- Qualified or comparative language about a sponsor's product or service;
- An endorsement;
- An inducement to purchase, sell or use the sponsor's product or service (other than the display of product at a sponsored event);
- Sponsor materials appearing in regularly scheduled and printed periodicals of an organization unrelated to the sponsored event; and
- Advertising payments contingent upon specific attendance levels at an event, broadcast ratings or other factors indicating a degree of public exposure.

(**NOTE:** Payments contingent solely upon the occurrence of the event are not subject to tax.)

For further details on this subject, contact the following references:

NCAA NEWS Federal Relations Office (202) 293-3050 and

WWW.IFEA.Com (Legislative Update Section).

Conclusion

These tax law changes determine how you should define corporate sponsorship - a change that should be reflected from the moment you pitch your sponsorship opportunity to a corporation up to, and including, the formalizing of the written sponsorship agreement you negotiate and execute. The IRS has given you (nonprofits) a break, so make sure you take advantage of it.

APPENDIX A
RECOMMENDED PERIODICALS

Advertising Age
Crain Communications, Inc., 360 North Michigan Street, Chicago, IL 60601, (312) 649-5200

Agent and Manager
Bedrock Communications, Inc., 650 First Avenue, 7th Floor, New York, NY 10010, (212) 532-4150

Amusement Business
BPI Communications, Inc., Box 1954, Marion Ohio 43306 (800) 745-8922

Electronic Media
Crain Communications, Inc., 360 North Michigan Street, Chicago, IL 60601, (312) 649-5200

Entertainment Marketing Letter
160 Mercer St., 3rd Floor, New York, NY 10012, (212) 941-0099

Event Marketer
33 South Main St., Norwalk, CT 06854, (203) 854-6730

Motorsports Marketing News
1448 Hollywood Avenue, Langhorne, PA 19047, (215) 752-7797

New York Daily News
Sports Column –450 W. 33rd Street, New York, NY 10001, (212) 210-2100

New York Post
Sports Column – 1211 6th AVE, New York, NY 10036, (212) 930-8000

New York Times
(Advertising Article, Section D), 229 W. 43rd Street, New York, NY 10036, (212) 556-1234

Promo
11 River Bend Drive South, P.O. Box 4225, Stamford, CT 06907-0225, (203) 358-9900

Sponsorship Report
IEG, 640 N. LaSalle, Suite 600, Chicago, IL 60610, (312) 944-1727

Sports Business Journal
Street and Smith's SportsBusiness Journal, 120 West Morehead Street, Suite 310, Charlotte, NC 28202, 704-973-1400.

Team Marketing Report
660 W. Grand Ave. Suite 100E Chicago, IL 60610, (312) 829-7060

The Downtown Reporter
215 Park Avenue South, Suite 1301, New York, NY 10003, (212) 228-0246

The Licensing Letter
160 Mercer St., 3rd Floor, New York, NY 10012 (212) 941-0099

The Sports Marketing Letter Companyr
89 Paul Place, Fairfield, CT 06430 (213) 259-3890
brianj1949@sportsindustry-daily.net

USA Today
Gannett Company, Inc., 7950 Jones Branch Drive ,McLean, VA 22107-3302 (703) 276-3400

Variety
249 West 17th Street, NY, NY 10011 (212) 337-6925

Wall Street Journal
512 7th Ave. Floor 6 NY, NY 10018 (212) 416-2000

BOOKS

Allen, Sylvia and Amann, C. Scott, ***How to Be Successful at Sponsorship Sales***, 732-946-2711.

Association of National Advertisers, ***Event Marketing: A Management Guide***.

Amshay, Thomas. ***Get Ready, Get Set, Get Sponsored***, self-published, RFTS Marketing and Consulting, Cuyahoga Falls, OH.

Connors, Tracy Daniel. ***The Nonprofit Management Handbook; Operating Policies and Procedures,*** John Wiley and Sons, Inc.

Embley, L. Lawrence. ***Doing Well While Doing Good***, Prentice-Hall.

Ernst & Young. ***The Complete Guide to Special Event Management***, John Wiley and Sons, Inc.

Gregson, Bob. ***Reinventing Celebration***, Shaman Publishing.

Harris, Thomas. ***The Marketer's Guide to Public Relations***, John Wiley and Sons, Inc.

Passman, Donald S. ***All You Need to Know About the Music Business,*** Simon & Schuster, New York, NY

Rapp, Stan and Collins, Tom. ***Beyond Maxi Marketing***, McGraw-Hill.

Rapp, Stan and Collins, Tom. ***Maxi Marketing***, McGraw-Hill.

Rapp, Stan and Collins, Tom. ***The Great Marketing Revolution***, McGraw-Hill.

Schreiber, Alfred. ***Lifestyle and Event Marketing***, McGraw-Hill.

Shemel, Sidney and Krasilovsky, William. ***The Business of Music,*** BPI Communications, Inc., New York, NY 10036

Schlossberg, Howard. ***Sports Marketing***, Blackwell Publishers, Cambridge, MA.

Stecckel, Dr. Richard and Simons, Robin. ***Doing Best by Doing Good***, Dutton.

APPENDIX B

OCEANFEST FACT SHEET

LOCATION: Promenade at The Ocean Place Hilton Resort and Spa, Long Branch, NJ

DATES/TIMES: July 4, 10am - 10pm

ATTENDANCE: 250,000+

AUDIENCE: All demographic groups with average attendees 30-45 years old, professional, married with children. Visitors come from all over New Jersey and metro New York.

SPECIFIC ACTIVITIES: Spectacular fireworks display
VIP reception and priority viewing ..."Evening Under the Stars"
Sports event
Entertainment ...bands, dancing, singing, performance art
Wide range of food selections
Quality arts and crafts

MARKETING OPPORTUNITIES: Radio, TV, and print coverage (value = $75,000)
Large street banners on Broadway, Joline, Norwood Avenues
Booth space
Audio billboards
Inclusion on posters, flyers, etc. (100,000+)
On-site signage
Table tents
New Jersey Monthly

PROMOTION IDEAS: Product sampling
Database development(register to win)
Product sales
Contest/promotions
Premium incentives
Couponing/bouncebacks
Cross-promotions/sponsor partnerships

SPONSORSHIP OPTIONS RANGING TITLE SPONSORSHIP TO BOOTH DISPLAYS LET US TAILOR ONE THAT WORKS FOR YOU!

A terrific opportunity to become involved in a community event that attracts over 250,000 people each year from all areas of New Jersey and the Tri-state. One of the premiere events on the Jersey Shore.

Allen Consulting, Inc. 732-946-2711

SAMPLE POST EVENT REPORT

OCEANFEST

POST EVENT REPORT 2004

Description	Impressions/Rate	Value
New Jersey Monthly ad	97,200 (10% of ad value)	$799.50
Asbury Park Press advertorial	221,450 @ $10/CPM	$2,214.50
Atlanticville advertorial	8,400 @ $10/CPM	$840.00
200 table tents	1,200,000 @ $75/CPM	$90,000.00
100 posters	300,000 @ $35/CPM	$10,500.00
2-ups	10,000 @ $35/CPM	$350.00
WJLK radio spots	10 @ $100/each	$1,000.00
10 VIP tickets	10 @$250/each	$2,500.00
TOTAL MARKETING VALUE:		**$108,204.00**

MEASURED MARKETING VALUE = $108,204.00

APPENDIX D

SAMPLE CONTRACT

SPONSORSHIP OPERATING AGREEMENT

AGREEMENT made this _____ day of _____, 2005, by and between **(RADIO STATION)**, a **(STATE)** corporation whose principle office is located at _____ **(MEDIA SPONSOR)**, and (Name of event), a **(STATE)** corporation whose principle office is located at _____ _____ **(EVENT)**.

This Agreement outlines the sponsorship relationship between **MEDIA SPONSOR** and **EVENT**. **MEDIA SPONSOR** agrees to provide **EVENT** with the following coverage:

- Radio remote from 6-9:30 pm on Saturday, July 4;
- 80 - :15 shared promotional announcements to run 6/25-7/2;
- :30 spots on (media) with sponsors names to run 6/25-7/2;
- :60 spots on (media) dedicated to event and sponsors to run 6/25-7/2;
- 20 - :60 spots on (media) to promote event and sponsors to run 6/25-7/2;
- Two :60 breaks per hour during live broadcast;
- Live simulcast of music accompanying fireworks display July 4th UNLESS there is conflict with the Red Bank simulcast).

The total value of this coverage is $14,500.00.

In return for said sponsorship, **MEDIA SPONSOR** receives the following sponsorship benefits:

- Official radio sponsor of **EVENT** with prominent logo identification on all printed materials as well as inclusion in **The Atlanticville** advertorial and COMCAST cable coverage/promotion;
- VIP privileges including 30 VIP hospitality tickets and 30 VIP parking passes;
- Prominent banner display at **EVENT** site;
- Inclusion on three street banners;
- One booth space on promenade;
- Right to sell two sponsorships from the sponsorship options program NTE $10,000 (If sponsorships are sold, **MEDIA SPONSOR** keeps sponsor dollars and provides **EVENT** with additional media value equal to sponsorship sale);
- Other benefits as deemed mutually acceptable (and outlined by addendum to this contract).

It is further understood and agreed that the conditions and agreements contained herein are binding on, and may be legally enforced by, the parties hereto, their heirs, executors, administrators, successors and assigns.

194

Neither **EVENT** nor **MEDIA SPONSOR** shall be liable for the failure to perform their obligations under this Agreement if such failure is due to acts beyond their control including, without limitation, acts of God, acts of the public enemy, acts of government, civil disobedience, lock out freight embargoes or any other cause or condition beyond the **EVENT**'s or **MEDIA SPONSOR**'s control.

All parties agree not to disclose to any other party any proprietary information acquired about the other. All parties further agree not to disclose, without prior written consent of **EVENT** and/or **MEDIA SPONSOR**, any information obtained about either party.

If, in the event of any dispute or controversy arising out of this Agreement, its performance or breach, and the parties to it are unable to settle the dispute themselves, such dispute shall be submitted to arbitration in _____County, (STATE). Arbitration shall be initiated by written notice by either party and shall be settled in accordance with the Uniform Arbitration Act as adopted by the State of_____, by a single arbitrator selected in accordance with the Rules of the American Arbitration Association from a panel of arbitrators provided by the American Arbitration Association who have experience with performance agreements. The decision of the Arbitrator shall be binding on both parties.

Agreed and accepted this _____ day of _____, 200_, by the undersigned.

For MEDIA SPONSOR   For EVENT

_____   _____
Date: _____   Date: _____

This contract contains some boilerplate that protects you, the event and the sponsor. Notice that it is quite precise about who does what and when. The tighter your contract the better your understanding and relationship with sponsors.

APPENDIX E   <u>Inventory/Pricing Matrix</u>

Inventory	Quantity	# of Impressions	Value	Total	Title	Presenting	Supporting	Associate				

Anatomy of an event ... case history

Planning an event seems like a simple enough concept. Start with an idea, hire some talent, put out a little publicity and - voila - you have an event. For any of you who have done events, you already know that it is never that simple. In this article you will be provided with a simple program for event design and management and, following that, a specific timeline for an event, from start to finish. A detailed presentation of an actual event, Oceanfest, a 4th of July celebration that features sand, water, food, crafters, children's games, sports (hoop-it-up, etc.), entertainment and, of course, fireworks, will be spotlighted. And, although this event attracts in excess of 200,000 people, the fundamentals are the same whether 500, 5,000, or 50,000 people attend.

WHERE TO START

Start with a goal, an objective. Why are you having the event? Who do you want to attend? Your primary objective might be to attract people to your community to demonstrate that it is a great place to live, work and play. A secondary objective might be to reinforce your positive image with current residents and business owners. A third objective could be to raise money. And, finally, remember to have fun!

When deciding on an event, do your homework. See what other communities, similar to yours, have done successfully. Look at your competition ... is another community, close to you, putting on a similar or competitive event at the same time? Look at your own community ... what can it support? Be honest with yourself; don't plan something so grandiose that it fails. You lose credibility (and money) and future events could be more difficult to produce or get community involvement. What resources are available to you (volunteers, paid staff, municipal services, etc.)?

Then, be creative. What would work in your community? For example, eight years ago Aitkin, Minnesota put on their first annual fishhouse parade. It was held the day after Thanksgiving and, for those of you who don't know what a fishhouse is, consisted of a variety of floats all centered around the houses that Minnesota fishermen build when fishing on the ice in the winter. (In fact, it's not just Minnesota but any Northern climate that has cold winters!). The reason for the parade? They thought that there should be something the day after the Macy's Thanksgiving Day Parade that was more local and indigenous to the area! Aitkin, by the way, has a population of less than 1,500.

The first year, 1991, there were probably only 200 people in attendance. They had 60 units in the parade and the majority of the parade participants were from Aitkin or the very close communities of Crosby, Brainerd, and Deerwood. However, through good public relations, community involvement, clever marketing ideas, media sponsors and regular sponsors, the event has grown to be recognized statewide and, last year, 15,000+ people crowded the parade route! Plus, there were more than 100 units in the parade and they came from a wider geographic radius than before. The moral of this story? They had an idea, they started small, they approached it professionally and built on it, year after year, until it reached its current level of success. Good advice for all event organizers!

WHEN TO START

Ideally, you should start planning your event one year in advance. This gives you time to solicit sponsors in a timely fashion, develop a strong volunteer organization and plan for success. In fact, once you have an event idea/plan/strategy in place your next step should be to get funding, whether it be through sponsorship, fundraising, grants, donations or municipal budget allocations. When soliciting sponsors be sensitive to their budget years and get to them *before* they start their budget planning process so you are included in next year's budget. One of the biggest mistakes consistently made by event organizers is waiting until the last minute before they start contacting sponsors. The reality? The shorter the lead time you give the sponsors the less money you will raise; conversely, the longer the lead time, the more sponsorship dollars you will generate for your event.

You should also start selecting your talent, soliciting food vendors and crafters, and recruiting volunteers. If you are having talent … singers, dancers, bands, clowns, performers of any type … book them early (six to nine months before your event). Freehold, New Jersey holds a series of summer concerts every year. Those concerts are booked nine months in advance of the season since many of the groups are popular Jersey Shore bands and would not be available if they were contacted on short notice. And, where do you find talent? Call your local arts organization, high school band directors and music teachers, local clubs and theatres, local organizations (such as Kiwanis, Chamber of Commerce, Optimists, etc.), and fellow Main Street Managers. Contact the **International Festivals and Events Association** in Boise, Idaho (208-433-0950) to find out if they have a local chapter and can give you some contact names. When booking your talent, take the audience composition into consideration. Are you doing family entertainment? Seniors? Boomers? Gen-X? Your talent mix will be different for each of these demographic markets.

If you are having food vendors and/or crafters, prepare your mailing at least nine months before your event. To attract more crafters, make sure your event is listed in **Sunshine Artists** as well as other local and regional event calendars. This allows you to reach people outside your market area that might want to participate in your event. Check out the various craft magazines at your local library and see which ones have event listings. Some of them are free; others charge a nominal sum for listings in their publications. For food vendors, always approach your local restaurants, delis and diners first. Remember, your job is to serve the local community and help those businesses. If, however, they don't want to participate, you can go outside your town for food vendors.

198

When recruiting volunteers look to your various service clubs within the community as well as church and civic groups. If you are working with a charitable organization … United Way, the local hospital auxiliary, Rotary, Kiwanis … look to their membership for volunteers. This is particularly viable when that organization has an opportunity to hitch hike on your event for fundraising of their own (selling t-shirts, hot dogs, raffle tickets, etc.). Develop a volunteer's workbook that carefully details the various volunteers needed and what their responsibilities will be. Don't overload your volunteers. It is better to have more volunteers, with each one doing a small bit, than a few volunteers who end up being overwhelmed with multiple responsibilities. The latter scenario leads to burn out and loss of a good volunteer.

WHO DOES WHAT

Ideally you would have a staff for event management and administration and a revenue-generating group. However, that's not the way it really is! What really happens is that you end up doing everything with, hopefully, a cadre of volunteers that can assist you.

- **Management and Administration**

Special events come in all sizes, from the simple car wash to raise money for the local church group to the Olympics. Though event sizes vary dramatically, the basic administrative and organizational components do not. In fact, organizing an event is very similar to setting up a small business. You need a plan with clearly defined goals and objectives, someone in charge, a budget and the operating plan (who is going to do what, when and where).

The major categories of an event are management and administration, revenue generation, and on-site management. Within each of these categories are subcategories of function and responsibility. Note, too, that many of the functions overlap, e.g. sponsorship can be undertaken by the event manager, marketing person or solely by someone designated to sell sponsorship (or all of them, depending on their skills and the needs of the event.)

a. *Event Manager*

The person responsible for the overall management of the event is the event manager. He/she is involved in event strategies, site negotiations, volunteer coordination, planning marketing strategy, determining the production time line, pre-event site surveys, talent selection and overseeing the day-to-day operation of the event staff.

b. *Volunteer Coordinator*

The volunteer coordinator is responsible for ensuring that there are enough volunteers to make the event function efficiently. Many of your volunteers can be drawn from the community at large through service organizations, churches, local charity groups, residents and your business community.

c. *Marketing*

The individual handling marketing is responsible for advertising and public relations, graphic design, production of collateral material (brochures, posters,

199

flyers, bag stuffers, payroll inserts, billing inserts, etc.), sponsorship sales, sales promotion, exhibit space sales, program book sales, and development of cross-marketing relationships (in the community with other groups or with multiple sponsors). This person is responsible for generating sponsorship dollars to support the event for helping to ensure that enough funds, beyond costs, are generated to make the event successful. (See Revenue Generation that follows for the many other ways you can raise money, in addition to sponsorship.)

d. *Finance*

The finance person is responsible for putting into place a system that effectively controls expenditures, as well as ensuring that income exceeds expenditures. (Works closely with the Event Manager and Marketing person in this particular revenue and expense area.) A simple numbered purchase order system, with two signatures for approval on ordering and a two-signature check payout system, are very effective in keeping an accurate accounting of expenses and revenues. With the general availability of computer spreadsheet programs, there is no reason that the finance person cannot update the income and expenses on a weekly basis. As in any business venture, this allows the management team to track and adjust the budget to accurately reflect changes in income and/or expenses.

e. *Legal*

Whenever you negotiate a relationship – celebrities, sponsors, venues, teams, entertainment, performers, other organizations – you need a contract. The contract should be prepared by a lawyer. This ensures that all major commitments are clearly defined and there is no room for future misunderstandings. The contract should very clearly define areas of responsibility, limitations, confidentiality or nondisclosure, indemnification, individual rights, and recommendations for an equitable resolution if a dispute arises. (For more details on specific contract elements, an excellent resource is **How To Be Successful At Sponsorship Sales**, published by Allen Consulting, Inc., Holmdel, NJ, 732-946-2711. 238 pages of vital sponsorship information including legal information - beyond sponsorship - written in simple, easy-to-understand language.)

f. *Insurance*

Just as you need legal safeguards, you need to have insurance protection. Insurance can protect you against greed, weather, accidents, violence, and human error. The types of insurance most common to special events include comprehensive, general liability, errors and omissions, accident, cancellation, spectator/participant coverage, sponsorship, workman's compensation, and weather. Several major insurance companies specialize in event insurance and can be contacted through your local insurance agent. Event insurance is usually expensive. However, when the extensive liability of the alternative is considered, one quickly realizes it is an essential investment (and component) of the event. Try to get your local community to add your event onto their

200

insurance. It will save you a lot of money and the cost to them is minimal as contrasted to your having to carry all this insurance.

- **Revenue Generation**

How does an event make money? One of the primary ways is to sell sponsorships. Sold in various dollar increments, sponsorships are designed to provide the sponsoring organization with an opportunity to support a worthwhile event while getting its message to its target customers and/or the public. The sponsor's target customers may include its own employees, consumers, others within the trade, and the media, to name just a few. Keep these realities in mind when selling sponsorships - understanding the reason sponsorship is being done helps you define a sponsorship program that helps a company achieve their stated objective(s).

Another way to generate revenue is to have a variety of activities with specific fees attached for participation. For example, participants pay a fee to compete, exhibitors pay a fee for display space, food vendors pay a fee to sell, parade participants pay a fee for placement, attendees pay a fee for photographs with celebrities, spectators pay a fee at the gate, and so on. (Ed. Note: Never work with vendors on a percentage unless you have a way of controlling the money such as tickets that the vendors have to turn in at the end of the event in order to get their money. With a flat fee, you are assured of getting your money!)

Yet another way is to have various collateral materials in which (or on which) people can advertise. These include a program book or some sort of commemorative piece, display boards (with sports these can be the scoreboard or leader board), event maps, event posters, etc.

Other ways of bringing in additional monies including having a carnival as part of your event, for which the proceeds are split 75/25 (75% to the carnival, 25% to you), a raffle with a 50/50 split, games of skill, electronic games, and so on.

As you do event marketing you will be using all of these activities to generate revenue for your event.

- **On-Site Management**

The function of this group is to see that sufficient planning and preparation have taken place to ensure a smooth-running event. Because the event occurs in "real time," with no rehearsal and no opportunities to do it again, all logistical issues and problems have to be solved, mentally, before they happen.

On-site management is responsible for such mundane, but necessary, items as the following:
- Portable sanitation facilities;
- Tents;
- Lighting;
- Security and crowd control;
- Audio systems;

- Fencing;
- Bleachers;
- Tables and chairs;
- Paper towels and toilet paper;
- Traffic control;
- VIP treatment;
- Banners and signage;
- Communications;
- Sponsor liaison;
- Food handling and distribution;
- Staging, lighting;
- In short, anything that is on-site!

On-site workers should do a pre-event survey to determine any problem areas and how to most efficiently lay out the event. Then, 12 hours before the event do another survey to ensure nothing has changed. On-site staff is usually at the event many hours before its official opening: tents, chairs, and other physical setups do not go up quickly (or easily!), and there are always last-minute details that need attention before the successful start of the event. They are also usually the last ones on-site, long after the event is over, tending to the cleanup operation and overseeing the return of all rented equipment. Their primary objectives are to return the site to its original pre-event condition and see that all contracted and purchased goods are returned intact.

TIME LINE
This timeline will be presented on a month-by-month basis to help you develop your own event strategy. Keep in mind that it is an *ideal* strategy; real world sometimes is different!

12 months before your event
- Develop your event strategy, set date, times and rain date;
- Decide what your event components will be (food? entertainment? rides? crafters? what?);
- Take inventory of your event ... what you have that will benefit sponsors and media partners; develop your sponsorship fact sheet; start soliciting media partners and sponsors.

11 months before your event
- Start your volunteer recruitment;
- Continue sponsorship solicitation;
- Develop media list with contact names, addresses, telephone numbers, e-mail addresses, fax numbers, deadlines, etc.;
- Develop your marketing plan (posters? flyers? banners? table tents? PR plan?).

10 months before your event
- Apply for community funding;
- Apply for all your permits (site, banners, etc.);
- Continue sponsorship solicitation;

- Send out first press release and public service announcement to print and electronic media, announcing event;
- Contact local, regional and national tourism offices to get onto their date calendars;
- Start soliciting talent if you are having entertainment;
- Prepare vendor solicitation forms (food, crafters, commercial displays);
- Place ads in **Sunshine Artists** and other crafter publications, notifying them of your event and how to get an application.

9 months before your event
- Develop an event handbook, who does what;
- Start volunteer training;
- Continue sponsorship solicitation;
- Solidify your media partnerships.

8 months before your event
- Contact fire, police, first aid and sanitation departments to explain event and get their cooperation/participation;
- Continue soliciting and selling sponsors;
- Do first vendor mailing (food, crafters).

7 months before your event
- Do second public relations mailing;
- Start contacting radio and TV for interviews to promote your event;
- Submit magazine articles re: your event;
- Do site survey.

6 months before your event
- Order tents, staging, sanitary facilities … all on-site materials needed to produce your event;
- Establish volunteer responsibilities;
- Do third press release;
- Develop event-specific website (hyperlink to your current site);
- Meet with current sponsors to discuss the involvement of **their** PR people.

5 months before your event
- Develop collateral material (posters, flyers, banners, table tents, etc.);
- Continue sponsorship solicitation;
- Complete talent negotiations and solicitations; mail contracts, deposit checks, confirmations to talent;
- Continue public relations activity.

4 months before your event
- Solicit PR material from sponsors, talent and vendors;
- Continue sponsorship solicitation;
- Continue public relations activity;
- Print all collateral material.

3 months before your event

- Do an event review ... what's missing? Not enough money? Not enough volunteers? Not enough vendors? Talent cancellations? Decide what areas need greater effort on your part.
- Continue sponsorship solicitation;
- Continue public relations activity.

2 months before your event
- Send sponsor, vendor, food and talent confirmation letters;
- Continue PR activity;
- Order volunteer t-shirts;
- Develop media partner's collateral material (if doing an advertorial, write copy for them; if radio partners, provide them with the appropriate sponsor tags and event copy; if cable or TV partners, provide them with event spots).

1 month before your event
- Put up street banner;
- Distribute collateral material;
- Put up table tents;
- Re-confirm talent;
- Increase PR activity;
- Meet with volunteers and give assignments;
- Re-confirm on-site support services (tents, sanitation facilities, staging, lighting, etc.);
- Re-confirm municipal services (police, fire, sanitation, etc.);

One day before your event
- Do final site survey and walk through;
- Re-confirm all services (tents, port-a-potties, etc.);
- If an outdoor event, check the weather channel;
- Alert local police and Chamber of Commerce as to contingency plan if bad weather;
- Pray!

Case History Using the Time Line

As stated earlier, this is an ideal time line, allowing you one full year to plan an event. If you plan multiple events, as many of you do, you have a number of time lines going at any given moment. Some activities can be combined for multiple events, which create greater efficiencies during the year; other activities have to be done individually. For example, once you have developed an event calendar you can sell some of your sponsors on multiple event participation; others may opt for a single event sponsorship. At least, when calling on the sponsor, you have options from which they can select. Another example of "bundling" you activities would be in negotiating for tables, chairs, and tents. If you can offer your vendor a number of opportunities, you can negotiate for a better price and, in some instances, get the vendor to make a donation. For example, a tent supplier to the Freehold Center Partnership recently donated 20 chairs for a specific event because the Partnership had spent in excess of $1,000.00 with this particular vendor in a year. The donation was worth $30.00 and saved the Partnership from having to pay for the chairs. Always remember to be creative in your thinking and your approach.

To demonstrate these event fundamentals, Oceanfest '99 will be used as a recent example of an event that was produced following the concepts previously discussed. As background, Oceanfest '99 was started in 1991 as an Independence Day celebration. It is the primary fundraiser for the Greater Long Branch Chamber of Commerce. Held in Long Branch, New Jersey, the event is held on the boardwalk promenade on the ocean, directly in front of the Ocean Place Resort and Spa. Consisting of crafters, vendors, sponsors, sports, entertainment, kiddy rides, food and a host of other activities, the event was always a one-day affair that attracted 200,000+ people annually. The event grew each year and, in 1998, it was decided that since July 4 was on a Sunday in 1999 and Long Branch had just successfully completed a beach replenishment program, the event would be increased to two days. The committee made this decision immediately after last year's event. Getting the city to support this decision took a little longer!

The biggest obstacle was expense. Since the city provide police, fire, first aid and sanitation services to the event they argued that they couldn't afford to double those expenses for a two day event. The event organizers asked if they provided a solution to that additional expense would Mayor and Council approve the additional day. They agreed.

It was decided that one way to generate additional money would be to put out a Request For Proposal (RFP) to all the soda companies for sales and service on the existing municipal vending machines (which were then all under different contracts). Developing the RFP, following the guidelines for municipal bidding, getting responses and determining who would get the contract took six months! In late January 1999, Mayor and Council approved the two-day event and passed a resolution approving it.

What did this do to the time line activities? Sponsorships were being sold on the basis that the event would *probably* go to two days; sponsorship dollar participation was based on two days; the media partnerships were based on two days … all done because the event organizers were confident that Mayor and Council, once they knew the monies could be recouped, would approve the two day event! However, talent couldn't be booked until the final approvals were received.

The minute the event was approved for two days, vendor solicitations were sent out, talent solicited (including a featured band for the beach concert) and booked, and suppliers contacted. Sponsors were solidified and contracts negotiated. It was decided to add more sandsculptors to the festivities (one had been featured in 1998) because it was a popular attraction and sponsors loved the concept of having their logos sculpted in sand. These sculptors were contacted and booked in February, six months before the event.

March and April were busy with public relations activity, solidifying media partners, soliciting and selling additional sponsors, processing vendor requests, and

205

working with new hotel management to ensure a smooth transition to a two-day event. All collateral material was designed including table tents, posters, flyers, payroll inserts, and - a major coup - large posters and promo pieces that were to be distributed by New Jersey Transit on all trains and busses. A five minute video was produced which would be aired on Newsmakers, an hourly insert (24/7) on the Comcast cable network.

The media partners for Oceanfest were Y-107, a local Long Branch radio station; the New York-based trio of WPLJ/Radio Disney/WABC; Comcast cable/CN8; the two-newspaper group of **The Atlanticville** and **The Coaster**; and the Asbury Park Press. The latter publications were to each produce an advertorial for the event with Allen Consulting, the event producers, providing editorial content. All editorial content was developed during May. In addition, radio spots were written and all sponsor radio tags were given to the appropriate media. Comcast/CN8 was provided with copy and graphics for a spot.

In June the site map was developed by the Chamber. Immediately upon completion of the map, all sponsor, vendor, food and talent confirmation letters were sent with instructions on where to park, when to show up, what their location was, etc. PR activity was dramatically increased. A web site was developed that would hyperlink to the city's web address. Three horizontal street banners - 4' x 25' - were put up across heavily trafficked streets. Table tents were put into participating restaurants and in every hotel room of the Ocean Place Resort and Conference Center. Payroll stuffers were inserted in 3,500+ Monmouth County employee paychecks. Plus, even though there was a beach, special sand had to be ordered and brought in for the sculptors!

Then, two weeks before the event, sponsors who hadn't been solicited began to call! The NBA Jam Van wanted to be there; Keebler Cookies wanted to be there; Nissan Motors wanted to be there! (Ed. Note: Never say "No" … just figure out how you can give them value on such short notice!). Talent began calling and re-confirming. A "sand tutorial" event was planned for the media the day before the event. Telephone calls, e-mails and faxes were sent to encourage the media to come and participate. Many promised to be a part of the festivities. (Ed. Note: Even when they say they will come, they may not. Don't be discouraged!).

What happened? The media event attracted a small number of participants; however, the pre-event coverage generated millions and millions of print and electronic media impressions. As a result, on Saturday, July 3, and Sunday, July 4, thousands of people showed up in spite of the fact that the temperature was almost 100°. The sandsculptors were the hit of the event with people lining the boardwalk to watch them work.

The event generated revenue in the low six figures and gave the Chamber a mid-five figure profit. In addition, it continues to be one of the major events at the Jersey Shore attracting hundreds of thousands of people to an event that offers a diversity of activities in a beautiful location.

APPENDIX G

EVENTS BENEFITS CHECKLIST

Let's look at this list and see what components are important to help you achieve your business objectives. We can then customize a program to meet your specific needs.

_____ Radio commercials
_____ Newspaper advertising
_____ Television
_____ Transit (bus and rail) cards
_____ Brochures
_____ Booth
_____ Participation in _____
_____ Volunteer recognition
_____ Banners
_____ Hospitality
      _____ Customers
      _____ Clients
      _____ Staff
      _____ Employees
_____ Sampling
_____ Product sales
_____ Audio announcements
_____ On-site signage
_____ Public relations
_____ Internet
_____ Sales promotion
_____ Database development
_____ Contests
_____ Premiums
_____ Cross-promotion with other sponsors
_____ Meet other sponsors
_____ Category exclusivity
Other: _____
_____
_____
_____
Based on this discussion, the best partnership would be the
_____. Let's walk
through that right now to ensure that we have met all your needs.

_____
"Name of Event ... contact information"

Index

211